The Ups & Downs of
UMBRELLAS

by
Brenda Stacey

Illustrated by
Richard Sawers

ALAN SUTTON

First published in the United Kingdom in 1991 by
Alan Sutton Publishing Limited · Phoenix Mill · Far Thrupp
Stroud · Gloucestershire

First published in the United States of America in 1991 by
Alan Sutton Publishing Inc · Wolfeboro Falls · NH 03896-0848

British Library Cataloguing in Publication Data
Stacey, Brenda
The ups and downs of umbrellas.
1. Umbrellas, history
I. Title II. Sawers, Richard
391.44

ISBN 0–86299–748–8

Library of Congress Cataloging in Publication Data applied for

Typeset in 10/11 Baskerville.
Typesetting and origination by
Alan Sutton Publishing Limited.
Printed in Great Britain by
The Guernsey Press Company Limited,
Guernsey, Channel Islands.

CONTENTS

ACKNOWLEDGEMENTS

The authors and publishers are grateful to the following for permission to reproduce material:

Preface by Max Beerbohm by kind permission of *Mrs Eva Reichmann; The Big Umbrella, Damon Runyon, Constable Publishers;* extract on page 83 *reproduced by permission of Curtis Brown, London, on behalf of Richard Gordon;* Ediciones Destino S A, Alvaro Cunqueiro, Merlín y Familia; extract from Barclay Wills' *The Downland Shepherds* by Gordon Beningfield, Richard Pailthorpe and Shaun Payne, Alan Sutton Publishing Ltd. Although considerable effort has been made to trace and contact original authors, this has not proved possible in every case. To those writers who have remained elusive, the compiler and publishers offer grateful acknowledgement for the extracts reproduced.

PREFACE

What is an Englishman without his umbrella? Take it from him, and you rob him of the staff he leans on through Life's pilgrimage. It is the Excalibur he brandishes in all battles – disarm him of it, and he is your prisoner. It is his crozier, sceptre, fairywand. It is the very plinth and emblem of all his majesty, and his soul is in its folds. Beer and Bible, according to his neighbours, are the explanation of him; but we who know him well know well that he depends on neither of these wholesome stimulants. It is the umbrella which has made Englishmen what they are, and its material is the stuff of which Englishmen are made.

MAX BEERBOHM

One

OPENING UP

N O MATTER how many religions the English do or do not have, or how many sauces, there is still only one topic of conversation: the weather. Strange, then, is it not, that there has been so little and late an interest in umbrellas. The Chinese, after all, have been at it since the eleventh century BC.

Perhaps it should be admitted that the first umbrellas were really parasols in that they were used as protection from the sun rather than the rain, yet such as were seen by French and English travellers in the late sixteenth and early seventeenth centuries were a great surprise to them. 'Have you seen a device which certain persons of rank in Spain and Italy carry or have carried (for them), less to protect themselves against flies than against the sun?' asked Henri Estiennes. With equal wonder, Thomas Coryat, royal hanger-on, buffoon and erstwhile scholar as well as traveller, wrote of his two great surprises in Italy, 'forks and umbrellaes'. 'The Italians . . . do always at their meals use a little fork when they cut the meat . . . seeing all men's fingers are not alike clean.' And, of the umbrellaes, 'These are made of leather, something answerable to the form of a little canopy and hooped in the inside with divers little wooden hoops that extend the umbrella in a pretty large compass.'

Opinion was not entirely favourable, however, for Coryat's compatriot and contemporary Fynes Moryson considered 'umbrels' more of a hazard than a benefit. What happened, he asked, to all that hot air that rose up inside them? Was it not detrimental to the health of the traveller? So concerned was he about the funnel effect that he sought advice from a physician. But the Spanish and the Italians didn't worry, and Ben Jonson described the lady who fell at the court of Spain 'i' the King's sight, along' as 'there she lay, flat spread as an umbrella.'

The French weren't long to see the benefits either, and John Evelyn bought his first umbrella in Paris in 1644.

One of the oldest English umbrellas is at Cartmel Priory. Some say that as long as an impossible four hundred years ago it was used to shelter the Holy Sacrament on its way to the poor. The English as a whole though went on ignoring umbrellas until around 1700. Some coffee-houses then equipped themselves with communal ones, as witnessed by an advertisement which appeared in *The Female Tatler* in 1709. 'The young gentleman belonging to the Custom House, that, for fear of rain, borrowed the Umbrella at Wills Coffee House in Cornhill of the Mistress, is hereby advertised that to be dry from head to foot on the like occasion, he shall be welcome to the Maid's pattens.'

Churches had communal umbrellas. Since 'the devil never misses an opportunity', parsons had to withstand all sorts of inclement weather when conducting burials, and throughout the eighteenth century it was not uncommon for there to be a parish umbrella kept specially for such occasions. Some were so large, and, if made of leather, so heavy that they were attached to poles that could be thrust into the ground alongside the grave. There cannot have been much hope for the devil at an early Victorian ceremony when a green oiled canvas brolly some 7 ft high and 5 ft in diameter formed 'a decent and capacious covering for the minister', but the occasion was described as 'in every respect a more fitting exhibition than the watch-box sort of vehicle devised for the same purpose and in some churchyards trundled from grave to grave wherein the minister and clerk stand.'

The umbrella for everyday people took a long time to establish. John Gay of *Beggar's Opera* fame had written in 1712:

> Britain in winter only shows its aid
> To guard from chilly showers the walking maid

but it was hardly true at the time, for it wasn't until Jonas Hanway came along that the umbrella had a real protagonist in England.

Officially, Jonas is described as a 'philanthropist and traveller'. Actually, he was paradox *par excellence*. He practically invented the umbrella as far as the English were concerned, yet wrote a treatise on *The Pernicious Custom of Tea-drinking*. 'Were they the sons of tea-suppers who won the fields of Crecy and Agincourt, or dyed the Danube's shores with Gallic blood?' he asked.

Jonas was born in Portsmouth in 1712. At seventeen he was apprenticed to a merchant in Lisbon and at thirty-one went off to St Petersburg as partner to merchant Mr Dingley. This Marco Polo of his age then ventured to the Caspian Sea only to get mixed up in a rebellion. Homeward bound he got attacked by pirates and laid low by fever, but, back in quarantine in St Petersburg two years later he heard news of his being a beneficiary under a will. Back home in 1750 he could indulge his philanthropic tendencies. He published a history of his travels, but became more famous for his work on the protection of chimney-sweeps and prostitutes. He wrote numerous treatises on the social issues of the day, including *The Reciprocal Duties of the Wealthy and Indigent*, but, paradox again, he opposed the naturalization of Jews. Dr Johnson commented that whereas Jonas 'acquired some reputation by travelling abroad (he) lost it all by travelling at home.' In 1788, two years after being buried at Hanwell, Jonas was honoured with a bust in Westminster Abbey, that 'lumber room of the larger and less successful statuary of the eighteenth century'. Carlyle described him as 'a dull worthy man' who was 'not always so extinct as he has now become.'

Almost coincidental with the start of Jonas's umbrella crusade, Colonel (as he then was) Wolfe was writing from Paris, where he had official leave of absence to take lessons in riding, fencing and dancing but was reputed to be seeing a great deal of Court and Society, 'the people here use umbrellas. I wonder that a practice so useful is not introduced into England.' But Jonas was ridiculed by street urchins and attacked by sedan chair carriers who saw the alternative protection of the brolly as a challenge to their business. 'An umbrella is a sure sign that one possesses no carriage,' said the Marquis of Caraecioli who, incidentally, was the gentleman who made the disparaging remark about the Englishman's religions and sauce. The whole idea was so slow to be accepted that in the late 1770s *The Westminster Magazine* printed a news item describing how the strange contraption worked. 'It is fastened in the middle of a long japanned walking cane with an ivory head. It opens by a spring, and is pushed up towards the head of the cane when expanded for use.'

Gradually though the battle was won.

The Revd Sydney Smith, who as a young man 'had no umbrella; they were little used and very dear', nevertheless included the umbrella among eighteen changes for the good which took place in England 'since I first began to breathe in it the breath of life.' For the curious, some of the other advances in his list were braces to keep his trousers up, the invention of steam which reduced the nine-hour sailing from Dover to Calais, the railway from Taunton to Bath, and gas lamps. The Revd Smith died in 1845 with only one ambition left, 'and that is to be Archbishop of Canterbury.' *He* obviously did not feel that the brolly 'defied the purpose of heavenly rain' as did many of its critics.

By the 1850s the English had gone so far as to adopt a practice similar to one the French had pursued nearly a hundred years earlier on the Pont Neuf – hiring out umbrellas at one end of the bridge and collecting them at the other. The London Umbrella Company opened a number of depots in the City of London and developed a sophisticated scale of charges including 9d for the first day, reducing to 6d for each subsequent day, and off-peak rates from 9 p.m. to 9 a.m.

The first patent taken out on an umbrella was in 1786, but once umbrellas were accepted there was 'product development' in a big way; over one hundred and twenty patents were filed in the 1850s alone. Among the more fanciful were pipes to drain the water into a receptacle on the rim, and a built-in lightning conductor. Ingenuity knew no bounds, but the basic brolly changed little after Fox patented the steel frame in 1852. The only significant structural development since then has been Hans Haupt's telescopic umbrella which came along in 1930. Patents continue to be filed at the rate of about twenty a year, the majority being technical – opening, closing and latching devices – but imagination is not totally dead as witnessed by the neck-and-shoulder clamp which leaves both the arms free. The hat-like umbrella with ribs radiating from a headband is, however, merely a development of the coolie hat, making one question whether the Chinese really needed all those umbrellas in the first place.

Raining or not, whatever shape, form or fashion, the humble umbrella is, however, a useful thing to have about. Archdeacon Grantly 'raised his umbrella and poked angrily at the disgusting notice . . . the iron ferrule caught the paper at a chink in the post, and tore it from top to bottom.'

The anonymous friend of the anonymous heroine in Katherine Mansfield's *Psychology* 'fumbled down among the ribs of a large old umbrella . . . such a good place to keep flowers out of the wind.'

Lobelia Sackville-Baggins, that 'redoubtable old bat', used her umbrella to resist arrest in *The Lord of the Rings* and to make off with hidden silver in *The Hobbit*.

Freud found the ferrule of his brolly useful to pick the lock of his door when he'd forgotten his key.

On the other hand, it has to be admitted that it took Jerome K. Jerome, George and Harris a quarter of an hour of yelling, stamping and waving their umbrellas before the young lady in the railway buffet at Crewe asked if there was anything they wanted.

Two

LOOKING AFTER THEM . . .

A DMIRAL CROFTS kept his umbrellas hanging up by the shrubbery door. 'A good place, is it not?' He appreciated that others felt the butler's room more suitable, for 'One man's way may be as good as another's, but we all like our own the best.'

The Victorians, who had a proper place for everything, invented the umbrella stand. In the 1850s, stands were simple wooden affairs, although their obsession with the Gothic meant a back bent to resemble the top of a church window; a plain rectangular bar held the brollies in place below. They were considered an essential enough item of household equipment to be illustrated in A.J. Downing's *Architecture for Country Houses*.

Such simplicity was not to satisfy the Victorians for long. Moreover, they were in to iron. 'What the Gout Stool is to the late Georgians, the What-Not, the Umbrella-stand, and the Chiffonier are to the mid-Victorians,' wrote Evelyn Waugh. 'The chief attraction is the almost infinite invention to which they give scope.'

The umbrella stand grew into a sort of dumb-valet. Hats on pegs at the top. Marble half-way shelf. Drawers for gloves and clothes brushes. Mirror for final inspection – and of course cast iron for ornament. A notable example shown at the 1862 International Exhibition was designed by a Mr Henry W. Mason and executed by a Mr William Roberts of the Northampton Lion Foundry.

Then there was one which looked like a dog sitting on a tree stump with fallen leaves around. All iron, of course. The dog held an (iron) whip in his mouth and from the top end of the whip two long (iron) cords formed circles to end in (iron) bows on either side of the animal's head. The visitor placed his dripping brolly through one of the circles and jabbed its ferrule into the fallen (iron) leaves.

Simplicity returned at the end of the nineteenth century

with plain mahogany stands looking rather like double towel racks. There was no drip tray, but with plenty of domestics perhaps the puddles were no problem.

As items of furniture, umbrella stands continued to be important. Stephen Potter listed among his childhood memories '*The Laughing Cavalier* who hung above the umbrella stand at No. 36', and Waugh was writing in 1938 of the Victorian stands still found in provincial hotels, their chief defect being an 'unusual combination of weight and instability' which gave them a tendency 'to fall forward upon the user'.

The current fashion for 'interior design', a trend for which many a station bookstall must be grateful, has led to much substitution of the real by the ridiculous. Gone are the days when one threw away the teapot whose lid was broken. Now it finds its way into the bathroom where it sports a bouquet of dried Constance Spry. Large articles with a hole in either top or bottom, according to whim, make admirable umbrella stands.

> The elephant, a noble beast,
> Is met with chiefly in the East,
> Also at Southsea, where Aunt Melisande
> Keeps its foot as an umbrellistande.

Less watertight would be Napoleon's hat. Surely he must have had more than one in his fifty-odd years; perhaps he was just a little conservative in matters of style. The somewhat eccentric Lord Northcliffe was apparently delighted to find it fitted his own large head – the right way up of course, or perhaps one should say the right way across. Nicholas Bentley on the other hand said that 'the hat had been canvassed from time to time by interested parties' for a number of possibilities, including a muffin dish and a font. The reader will not be too surprised that the umbrella stand features on the list even though 'the front could be folded up to form the thing into a watering can.'

THE PROPERTY OF ST. AUGUSTINE'S

Three

... AND LOSING THEM

BSENT-MINDEDNESS may lead to the loss of a good many umbrellas, but borrowing is responsible for the loss of many more.

> Rainy days will surely come,
> Take your friend's umbrella home.

The fact that so many are borrowed may be among the reasons for

> The rain it raineth on the just
> And also on the unjust fella,
> But chiefly on the just because
> The unjust steals the just's umbrella

attracting more claims to authorship than Anon himself might muster. Anon is frequently attributed in this case, but Charles, Baron Bowen, who lived from 1835 to 1894, gets most votes. Others in the running include Sir George Bowen (no relation), Dean Swift, who 'lay a'bed till 11 o'clock thinking of wit for the day', Samuel Butler, Cynicus (on this occasion a Mr Robertson of Fifeshire) and a Bishop of London. Wellington would probably have cast his vote for the Bishop for it was the Duke who said that 'The Kildare Club can do what it likes (about membership) but if they let the bishops in, they had best look to their umbrellas.'

Evidence of the apparent exemption of umbrellas under the terms of the eighth commandment led A.G. Gardner to write an essay on '*Umbrella Morals*'. 'Quite impeccable people, people who would ordinarily seem unspotted from the world, are afflicted with umbrella morals,' akin, he said, to forgetting to return books and taking a rise out of the railway company by travelling first class with a third class ticket. The same people would never be found putting their hands in the pocket of another, forging a cheque or robbing a till.

Such moral laxity cannot be explained by the fact that it is raining and people fear for their persons or paraphernalia. There are essentialists, like Robert, who, having come out without his umbrella found himself 'umbrellaed to the gills. What had caused me to take up the one that had been leaning against the seventeenth-century chair I cannot say, unless it was the primeval instinct which makes a man without an umbrella reach out for the nearest one in sight, like a flower groping towards the sun.'

Then there are those like Psmith with ulterior motive plain. Leaving 'the window of the smoking room and having made his way with smooth dignity to the club's cloakroom, [he] proceeded to submit a row of umbrellas to a close inspection before selecting the best' to take across the road to shelter the 'sumptuously upholstered' Eve Halliday.

Helen just did 'nothing but steal umbrellas'.

No two people who lose their umbrellas to the ill-gotten gains of others react in the same way. According to Thomas Hardy, the inhabitants of Dorchester were so sanguine about the possibility of losing theirs, even from their own hallways, that they left their cottage doors open on summer days.

No wrath from the gods comes to members of the church – who must be among the most practised both in the art of borrowing and the most practised upon. A Canon of Durham pinned a punning verse up in the Athenaeum about the loss of a mere umbrella when it had been taken by Dean Lake.

Mr Pooter suffered everybody and everything and sustained only by belief in himself just went on his way out into the pouring rain when all he could find in the hall was a stick which Sarah said 'didn't belong to nobody'.

But, sorrowing Old Bassett said Robert's behaviour was 'the sort of thing that made a man sick at heart.'

Walderwick, totally unimpressed at the prospect of ranking with Sir Philip Sydney and Sir Walter Raleigh, was enraged at Psmith's action, while Mr Perrin rose to a 'trembling passion', not least because the 'rain was lashing against the window panes as though it had some personal grievance against him' and factotum Robert, who tried to be helpful, had seen only 'Miss Maddox's pink parasol' and that was last week.

If it's someone else's umbrella which is lost, reaction is again different. Traill thought it 'too absurd that a man mightn't take another man's umbrella', but then he was an

interested party since he had not only taken Perrin's but lost it as well. Moreover it was 'just the sort of umbrella with its faded silk and stupid handle that Perrin would be likely to have.'

Dr Johnson, a disinterested party, complained that Mrs Thrale lamented too loudly over hers when 'the world is bursting with sin and sorrow.'

A.J. Wentworth BA saw a want of sensibility in his headmaster who couldn't understand that the sensible thing for him, A.J. Wentworth BA, to be doing at eleven o'clock on a fine night was to be looking for his umbrella in the gamesroom cupboard which held 'cricket bats in winter and footballs in summer'. But then he was very particular about where he kept his umbrella; if it wasn't in the usual corner of the hall of his cottage, then he could expect to find it in the bedroom. The fact that he couldn't find it at eleven o'clock when he didn't need it – it wasn't raining and he had nowhere to go – disturbed him greatly. The nocturnal visit to the gamesroom cupboard ended in his stepping back on a cricket ball, smashing his torch against the wall and reeling back in the pitch darkness with Gilbert's fishing line unreeling about him. The insensitive headmaster was as disturbed as he, though for different reasons.

Misappropriation is a microcosm of life itself; there are winners and losers. Gardner lost on the occasion when 'the frame would not work, and if it had worked I would not have put the thing up for I would no more be seen under such a travesty of an umbrella than Falstaff would be seen marching through Coventry with his regiment of ragamuffins.' The Revd Francis Kilvert was however delighted when 'no sooner had Lady Hertford and her party gone than I found she had taken my umbrella and left me a much better one. A fine silk umbrella in place of my zenilla!'

There are those who try to right the wrongs. How could Gardner do otherwise? After dinner with politicians at some rich man's house, he was 'humbled by the magnificence' and 'terrified by the presence' of the umbrella he later found in his possession. He felt as though he had been 'caught stealing the British Empire'. How he would have envied Brahms 'who for all his grumbling and grizzling had never known what it felt like to be suspected of stealing an umbrella.'

Helen's attempt to put matters right was less happy. The

24

young man had been a little uneasy about raising the matter in the first place, but Helen was 'so very sorry. Do come in and choose one. What about this umbrella? No, it's all gone along the seams. It's an appalling umbrella. It must be mine.'

Father Brown only nearly lost his 'large, shabby umbrella' which constantly fell on the floor of the train. He went back for it while the train was still in Stratford station, but many travellers are less mindful and the man in the Lost Property Office got tired of being constantly interrupted while trying to eat his sandwiches. Two regular travellers on the 9.25 from Little Woking, 'one pale, tall, in a grey suit and a black bowler', the other 'short, red, in a brown suit and grey trilby' came in with monotonous regularity. Neither was able to complete the standard questionnaire on 'peculiar marks', so each in turn was awarded an umbrella which had been handed in and the other recommended to return in two days' time. Each did, often; in fact both did, often, and at the same time. Unable to bear it any longer, and no doubt hungry as well, the man in the Lost Property Office, according to Raymond Stephenson, 'fought back his sobs' and solved the problem by tying an iron paperweight around the brolly and throwing it out of the window into the river below.

Perhaps it is remarkable that we have a tale to tell at all for Mrs Elsie Strong, a descendant of Jonas and beneficiary of an umbrella belonging to him had to report in 1895, 'The umbrella, I deeply regret to say, is lost.'

Four

ESSENTIAL

P AGO-PAGO is reputedly the wettest place in the Pacific, but it is at least hot. There is therefore little which is essential other than the umbrella, as Dr Macphail found. The natives were 'clad in nothing but lava-lava'. Even that mini-skirt of the early 1900s was unheard of until the decent-minded missionaries came along.

The umbrella has also been found essential in climes which might have been expected to be more balmy. Zola found 'the truest friend he had was his umbrella' when staying in Bordeaux to feast on the succulent Arachon oysters. Clement Freud found 'a carriage attendant holds an umbrella over your head as you emerge from the taxi' at Reid's Hotel in Madeira. An example of the totality of the service no doubt, although one can't help hoping that the Tourist Board will forgive him. In his defence, it *was* November.

Some even use their grey brollies to shield them from the sun. Witness Sir George Sitwell, who, laying out the gardens at Renishaw, had some wooden towers constructed 'like an early machine for siege warfare or a drawing by Piranesi'. He spent a long time aloft 'with a large grey hat or grey umbrella to shield his light coloured skin and eyes from the sun.'

As essential as the brolly may be in all sorts of weather, what the much-derided Jonas could never have anticipated was its essentiality to men of fashion – 'Fashionable men are wedded to them', reported *The Tailor and Cutter* in 1895 – let alone the respectability bestowed on the carrier. 'It is the habitual carriage of an umbrella that is the stamp of Respectability. The umbrella has become the acknowledged index of social position,' wrote Robert Louis Stevenson. Was this too inherited from the East? Marco Polo had noted that Kublai Khan always had to have a brolly carried over his head when he went riding 'in token of his exalted rank'. J.W. Palmer, who travelled *Up and Down the Irrawadee*, commented that the 'inseparable gold umbrella . . . denoted the grandee as the star and garter does in England.'

Actually, Stevenson wasn't quite right about the index, since in England the umbrella transcended social class; the ubiquitous brolly became the antithesis of that other peculiarly English thing – class distinction.

When William, second porter at Maynard's the draper's was courting Jane, her employers were sceptical of his intentions even though 'his eminent respectability was vouched for by an alpaca umbrella from which he never allowed himself to be parted.' Once William got promoted to head porter at twenty-three shillings a week, he bought himself 'a new silk hat, yellow gloves, and a *new* umbrella'. He also found a new girlfriend.

George Borrow had found the cachet useful when, as an Englishman, he was trying to buy a pint of beer in a Welsh pub. 'Who doubts that you are a respectable character provided you have an umbrella?'

As a philanthropist, Jonas might have been pleased to learn how essential the umbrella could be as a means of disguise, particularly to one such as Mr Blackman of Hong Kong who used 'an ancient umbrella, green with mould' to disguise his growing lameness. As a true Englishman Jonas might have been flattered by Professor Pesca's 'gratitude to the country which afforded him asylum' after he left Italy for political reasons, but on the other hand Jonas may have felt Pesca's compliment of 'invariably carrying an umbrella' a little overdone and 'the gaiters and white hat' even more so.

The much disguised 5th Duke of Portland had much in common with the late Mr T.C. Druce of 68 Baker Street, including the fact that both had skin ailments which made them wish to avoid sunlight. Indeed, so much had they in common that Mrs T.C. Druce claimed that her husband was not dead at all but lived on in the 5th Duke. The case she brought in 1907 was ridiculed and Mr Druce successfully exhumed. The Duke's obsessive desire for secrecy, both before and after the trial, led to some peculiar habits, included in which was his hiding under his umbrella. Less successful for hiding from others though no doubt more than adequate in hiding from himself were the three frock coats he would sometimes wear on top of each other and the two-foot-high hat on top of one of the wigs from his large collection.

It is the very Englishness of the umbrella though which makes it so essential to the English character. Pendennis regarded his umbrella cases, note the plural, as one of the 'elaborate necessities of the English traveller', along with his dispatch boxes, guide books and passport. Galsworthy's *Gentleman* was 'that rather rare thing, a pureblood Englishman, having no strain of Scotch, Welsh or foreign blood in his pedigree for four hundred years at least.' He was never without his umbrella, even on the finest days, although 'the ferrule, from his habit of stumping it on the pavement, had a worn and harassed look and was rarely more than half present.'

As the ultimate complement to character, the umbrella again transcends class. Boz's clerk, who 'awakened no sympathy in the heart of any person, felt no pain, no pleasure . . . always carried one to the office in the morning.' And, not so long ago, when Miss Baker went out to look for the Lord, 'she put on her white straw hat with a broad brim and daisies round the crown. She took her umbrella, saw that the gas was turned off and that her key was in her bag and every window closed, and went out.'

Somehow, one cannot help feeling that it was more important that someone invented the umbrella than the weather.

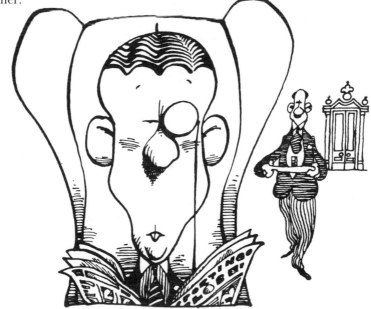

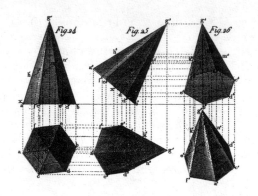

Five

UNUSABLE

DEBRETT'S *English Gentleman* states the rules quite clearly – 'A gentleman may carry a carefully rolled umbrella but never thinks of opening it . . . many gentlemen have never unrolled their umbrellas since they bought them.'

Thus it has always been.

Jonas was in trade, so he wasn't a gentleman, even though John Pugh's biography quoted in *The Penny Magazine* in 1836 said, 'When it rained, a small parapluie defended his [Jonas's] face and wig; thus he was always prepared to enter any company without impropriety or the appearance of negligence.'

In the 1780s, that arbiter of taste, *Town and Country Magazine*, referred to dandies, who of course may not have been gentlemen, as having umbrellas 'constantly under their arms'.

Beau Brummel's brown silk was renowned for its ever-present silk cover.

Emerson wrote of 'The Englishman [who] walks in pouring rain, swinging his closed umbrella like a walking stick.'

'Closely rolled umbrellas will be seen more frequently than ever before', said *The Tailor and Cutter* in 1895.

There must have been times when the weaker were tempted; after all, the author of '*Umbrella Morals*' did say his story was about 'how we play hide and seek with our conscience.' An ambiguous minute in the Royal Society's *Philosophical Transactions* for the year 1787 states, 'If the weather be rainy, an insulated umbrella may be carried in one hand.' Is 'carry' here synonymous with 'put up', or does it really mean 'carried'? Perhaps the matter was left for each to decide for himself, no vote being taken at the proceedings. Some hundred years later, one umbrella manufacturer actually recognized that a little cheating might go on in the rain – though most certainly not at the card table – and introduced a hollow walking stick whose head unscrewed to reveal 'the slimmest ever umbrella'.

There was little need to get the rules firmly sorted out though until the question of U and non-U became important. Christopher Sykes found a true English compromise. 'It is thought a fitting thing to wield an umbrella in the streets of London, but unspeakably non-U for the same man to wield it in country fields unless he be a clergyman.' One would expect clergymen to be gentlemen – though the Duke had doubts about some bishops – but such behaviour on their part is perhaps excused on the grounds of their still necessary attendance at funerals.

Jilly Cooper came to much the same conclusion at the end of the 1970s in her examination of *Class*. Henry Stow-Crat, 'for whom it was a point of pride at forty [that] he was able to get into the same pair of trousers and coat he wore at Eton', was naturally 'very conservative in his dress', and never carried 'an umbrella in the country'.

Cooper, however, allows special dispensation not only to the clergy but also to a gentleman 'where a woman might be dressed up and need cover.' Relaxation of the rules was not cognizance of characters such as Captain Wentworth but made on the grounds that 'on the moors they [women] can drown.' In case that suggestion is derived from personal experience, it would be inadvisable for every Thomas, Richard and Henry to assume that he is included among admissable opener-uppers.

The country is not the only place where a gentleman may not use his umbrella.

Jerome K. Jerome was finding it extremely difficult to know what to write in his diary the day after he saw the Passion Play at Oberammergau. His companion, B, suggested that the weather would make a suitable topic. Now, that was not because B was a 'true Englishman' to whom the weather would make a suitable topic. He suggested it because 'it rains at Oberammergau three days out of four, the reason that it does not rain on the fourth day being that every fourth day is set apart for a deluge.' Moreover, the theme had potential for development. 'Then you can comment on the hardihood of the Bavarian peasant. How he or she walks about bare-headed and bare-footed throughout the fiercest showers and seems to find the rain only pleasantly cooling. How during the performance of the Passion Play they act and sing and stand about upon the uncovered stage without taking the slightest notice of the downpour of water that is soaking their robes and running from their streaming hair to make great pools upon the boards; and how the audience in the cheaper unroofed portion of the theatre, sit with equal stoicism watching them, no one ever dreaming even of putting up an umbrella – or, if he does dream of doing so, experiencing a very rude awakening from the sticks of those behind.'

Umbrellas may be essential to the audience in the cheaper seats at any open-air performance as rib-diggers, but they are totally unusable for the practical purpose for which they were invented.

Unusable too, now that psychology has been invented, is the sort of umbrella the pious William Cowper described:

> We bear our shades about us, self depriv'd
> of other screen, the thin umbrella spread . . .

Every warrior possessed a wooden bowl, a fan, and an umbrella, and many also had brought iron swords and leather shields.

ERNEST BRAMAH
Kai Lung Unrolls His Mat

The tuck'd up sempstress walks with hasty strides
While streams run down her oil'd umbrella's sides.

JONATHAN SWIFT
Description of a City Shower

An umbrella of perfumed leather with gold fringe about it, which I brought out of Italy.

Bequeathed in the will of Robert Toft (1618)

During Townsend's Regatta at the siege of Al-Kut in the First World War, the 17th Indian Infantry Brigade advanced against the Turks in flat-bottomed boats. Bringing up the rear was the Medical Officer, seated beneath a large umbrella and hugging a block of ice.

The cane or closed umbrella should be borne as close to the body, as near to the front, as possible, and constantly in a perpendicular position.

J.S. DUNCAN
Hints to the Bearers of Walking Sticks and Umbrellas

... tempestuous clouds that stretched down in umbrella-like points towards the horizon.

DUFFERIN

... landscape lovingly umbrellaed by smiling clouds that took turns in the task of keeping the direct sunbeams from our faces.

BEARD

Six

IMAGINARY

T HE first nice thing about dreams is that they are easy to dismiss if you'd rather not remember them. You can put them down to indigestion.

The second is that you can interpret them as you wish, for nobody can tell you with any certainty what they mean. Whole books have been written on the subject, and if you decide to have one in your library you'd better have them all so that you can choose the interpretation you prefer. Some people may like the definition that dreaming of an umbrella means security. Some welcome it as a sign of fertility, although the very prospect of fertility may well give others further sleepless nights.

If it's security you need, don't worry if the brolly is torn. All that the tattiness means, according to one source, is that your security is just going to be a bit further ahead than you'd really like, but everything will be all right in the end. Not so another source, which says that a torn umbrella means that you are to be misunderstood and maligned! You may also be misunderstood if the brolly you are carrying is not your own. The man who dreamt up that one must have been reading *Hamlet*, for to dream of lending an umbrella is not to be recommended either – it leads to false friends. Others interpret lending as a charitable act. Losing one is indicative of your being in for a hard time at work. Giving an umbrella as a present may lead to your coming across somebody you haven't seen for years.

It's all right to dream of carrying your own umbrella even if it is not raining, for it means pleasure and prosperity to come, but if you see other people carrying theirs, someone is going to come to ask you for money. Dreaming of a closed umbrella shows your distrust of someone close to you. The nicest dream of all is of an open umbrella for it is your very own character reference – you have an open mind and adapt easily to both people and things about you.

Superstitions aren't any easier to explain – there's nothing so simple in umbrella lore as the cautionary tale of not walking under a ladder while the man above has a pot of paint in his hand. Opening an umbrella indoors is said to bring misfortune either on the do-er or the whole household. This is believed to originate from ancient worship of the sun in the East. Sunshades, so it is said, were sun-shaped so that the sun itself was not insulted by their use. Others might say that the circle just seemed a sensible shape to ward off the circle of the sun, but never mind.

Yorkshiremen, but only Yorkshiremen for some strange reason, should never put a brolly on a bed, for tragedy will follow. A quarrel will ensue if anyone puts one on a table, while an umbrella laid on a prompter's table is as doom-laden as Macbeth. It's also an unlucky thing to give as a present.

There's a good choice of beliefs should you drop your umbrella. The pessimist believes his mind will give way; the optimist that he will soon meet a friend. Nobody should pick up his own, any more than his own gloves, for a decision will then go against him. Pick up somebody else's, then there will be a decision in your favour. If American women pick up their own fallen brollies, they are likely to remain spinsters all their lives.

There's a nice little story of a superstition leading to invention. Jupiter was, among other things, god of thunder. So, when the English were still a bit unsure about the wisdom of carrying umbrellas at all and worried lest they would be struck by lightning if they did, the best umbrellas had acorns carved on their handles for protection. The oak tree was sacred to Jupiter and acorns were his symbol.

Jupiter wasn't the only god to get mixed up with umbrellas.

The Indian fertility specialist, Varuna, had one, and being a pretty sophisticated thinker used the brolly as a symbol of the importance of both sun and rain. Nearer home, Persephone had one too, and for much the same reasons.

For more vivid imagination, turn once more to the Chinese. Their tale is of the four Diamond Kings of Heaven, the brothers Mo-li Hung, Mo-li Ch'ing, Mo-li Hai and Mo-li Shou, their names meaning vastness, purity, sea and age. Their characteristics didn't tie up with their names though for Ch'ing was the tall one, standing some 24 ft in his socks; Hai had a guitar with which he could either stop the whole

universe or cause his enemies to burst into flames according to whim; Shou carried two whips and a bag containing a white rat, a snake or a striped marten, the last of which, with no trouble at all, could turn into a man-eating elephant.

Hung was the umbrella man. His umbrella had spiritual powers. Open, it could shroud both heaven and earth in total darkness. Held upside down, it brought on violent storms and earthquakes.

All four brothers died in battle when they came to the aid of the House of Shang. Early victory was theirs, and they ate and drank well. While comatose, the enemy attacked, and amid all the confusion Hung's umbrella was stolen. Enemy Huang T'ien Hua used his magic spike, known colloquially as the Heart Piercer, to stab one of the brothers in the neck and two others, including umbrella-man Hung, in their hearts. Survivor Shou thrust his hand into his bag, but, instead of finding his man-eating elephant, he found the enemy in disguise. The enemy not only bit off Shou's hand but rose to slay him.

Happier by far is the tale told by Galician Alvara Cunqueiro, although even here there is doubt as to a totally satisfactory outcome.

The Bishop of Paris sent messengers to Merlin with baggage 'carefully wrapped and secured by seven pieces of string' and so precious that the young servant stayed as close 'as a nun does to her beads'. Opened, the parcel revealed three umbrellas, one white with a black handle, one yellow with a silver handle, and one crimson with gold. Merlin doubted whether even the Pope had better. 'The white one, as you know,' he said, 'is called "Sun-come-out" and when you open it on the day of the Assumption of Our Lady in August, even if it's rainy at the time, you have a guaranteed sunny morning for the procession. The yellow one is called "Marvels", and it's a mighty secret gadget; you use it only at Whitsun, and when your Bishop is under it, he can speak and understand any language; even a dumb person can make his confession and your Bishop can hear him. As for the crimson one, well, that's used when you travel by night, and when you open it even on the darkest night you can see as if it were day. It's not really a parasol, more of a paradark, and its name is "Bright Star".'

Merlin's assistant considered his master as fine an umbrella repairer as the one at Orense. Merlin had mended the crimson one before when it belonged to Lancelot, although 'I didn't get it quite right ... and instead of helping you to see as if it were day, you couldn't see anything at all, not even the lamps that were lit.'

On this occasion Merlin decided not to charge – the repairs were minimal with only one weak rod and one detached requiring attention. 'Tell your Bishop that I won't charge him anything for the repairs, but next Whitsun, when he opens the yellow umbrella, he's to pay special attention to the language of magic, particularly the name of the metals and precious essences, because I want to finish reading one of the books about occult sciences that I have here, one that contains all the lore of the Chaldeans. And tell him not to waste the powers that "Bright Star" has by going to look for buried treasure in caves and ruins, because this umbrella was not made for that; it was made so that its owner can follow the steps of Jesus Christ our Lord, by night, along the road to Emmaus.'

Seven

SHADY PRACTICES

O SCAR WILDE defined depression as 'a wet Sunday on the Cromwell Road', and it was a wet Sunday afternoon in London in 1871 which caused French critic and historian Taine to exclaim, 'The few passers-by under their umbrellas in the desert of squares and streets have the look of uneasy spirits who have risen from their graves.' More of a comment on a Victorian Sunday perhaps than a deep reading of character, but scarcely more jolly than two of the three types of umbrella carrier that Robert Louis Stevenson found: hypochondriacs, who feared that getting wet led to colds, chills and rheumatism, and the frugal, fearing for their clothes. Those in his third category, fops and fools, would hardly have felt more flattered.

Any big city on a rainy day is fertile ground for study. Showery rather than consistently wet weather is better, for then there is a chance to study both the furled and unfurled.

One of the commonest uses of the furled by both the man of means and the expense-account executive is as a taxi-stopper. He of middle-management is less sure of his status and so more agitated in his ploy. He sees a taxi in the distance and is disturbed lest someone beats him to it. He jumps one foot into the gutter, raises his brolly and prods the sky in quick successive jabs as indeed he might wish to prod the boss who refuses to leave dead man's shoes. His rhythmic conducting is of the celestial choir of the gods, echoing his earthly prayer.

Then there is the clerk, standing in the bus queue. Someone said 'to see a London bus queue in the rain is to see a non-protest demo you could scarcely equal elsewhere', though if it's raining and the umbrellas are up, it is surely more reminiscent of a giant crocodile with pimples on its back. The clerk is resigned to a long wait as he is resigned to so many things. His knees are crossed, and between showers he leans on his flagging, unrolled umbrella as though it were a third leg. Waist down, he looks like a sort of wigwam.

Along comes the cyclist. When it's not actually raining, the city cyclist straps his (furled) umbrella to the back carrier. The ferrule thrusts rapier-like beyond the wheel, as demanding of a red flag as the forefront of the early Morris. The peasants of northern Portugal manage much better, with one hand on the handlebars and the other holding brolly aloft, but then the Portuguese have had more time to practise. They have had umbrellas much longer. Even Jonas had noted that 'they seldom travel without cloak and umbrella.'

The city walker is like the country tramp who shouldered his possessions in a red-spotted handkerchief. The metropolitan brolly is held handle down with ferrule against the shoulder dangling the ubiquitous plastic bag from the supermarket.

The stroller in the park jabs the ferrule of his brolly into the empty cigarette pack – and then doesn't know what to do with his prize.

The countryman up to town for the day, still in his deerstalker hat and looking cross because his appointment is too early for a cheap-day-return, carries his gingham as gun, through both habit and mood.

The young tourist has his house packaged on his back. Bedding bulges, pots and pans dangle. Less well accoutred than the compleat snail, he nevertheless fixes his brolly with ferrule aloft, an aerial tuned to direction.

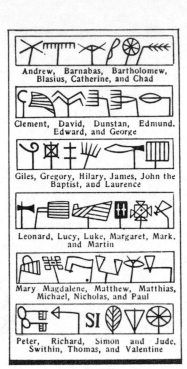

Andrew, Barnabas, Bartholomew, Blasius, Catherine, and Chad

Clement, David, Dunstan, Edmund, Edward, and George

Giles, Gregory, Hilary, James, John the Baptist, and Laurence

Leonard, Lucy, Luke, Margaret, Mark, and Martin

Mary Magdalene, Matthew, Matthias, Michael, Nicholas, and Paul

Peter, Richard, Simon and Jude, Swithin, Thomas, and Valentine

Eight

VENERATED

T HE patron saint of the French umbrella industry is most unlikely to have met with the object at all, for, although he lived to be almost a nonagenarian, he died around AD 560.

How then, did he, St Medard, get involved? Some say that as a young man he sheltered an eagle from a heavy rainstorm, but they do not tell how. Others say that it was not until the twentieth century that the French realized their industry had no protection other than the product, and during the year they came to consider the vacancy it just happened to start raining on 8 June, St Medard's day, and continued to do so for many weeks. Moreover, St Medard happened to be free, being occupied with little other than the prayers of those who suffer from toothache. Any painful association is counteracted by his feast day being celebrated with the proclamation of the most exemplary girl in the village who is then crowned with roses and given a purse of money.

Not a great deal is known about St Medard except that he was born of noble parentage. He had a twin brother Gildard. Both brothers entered the church and both became bishops, Medard of Vermand and Gildard of Rouen. King Clothair visited Medard on his deathbed, asked forgiveness for wrongs done unto Medard and built a basilica in his memory.

The English, who took a long time to catch up with the French as regards umbrellas at all, still have no such saintly cover. Should it be deemed desirable to fill the post, St Swithun comes to mind, although his association with rain rests solely on the fact that on the day his remains were transferred to holy ground, some years after his death, the deluge that occurred was said to be a show of his displeasure at all the fuss. He might have preferred to be remembered for returning to their shells the eggs some poor wench dropped as she crossed the Itchen.

Saints have a lot in common with statues – there are a lot of them both and neither is necessarily a permanent appointment. Saints may be discredited by papal decree and statues by seagulls or gunpowder.

In England there are only two statues which carry

umbrellas. George William Palmer and Sir Henry Waterlow was each erected by public subscription and each, strangely, during the subject's lifetime.

Each was a businessman, philanthropist, and Liberal MP. Each must have represented quite a challenge to his sculptor. Swords were inappropriate. So were horses. Neither aspired to the robes and regalia of the lords. Pedestals of baroque nymphs were no longer in fashion. It is no surprise that each ended up with what has been described as 'a restful hold of the coat near the collar in accordance with a familiar English habit.'

Mr Palmer was Mayor of Reading in 1889. He marked the occasion with the gift of twenty-one acres to the community for recreational purposes. As a Quaker, recreation meant activity, and the one condition of his gift was that no intoxicating liquor should be allowed in the new park. His munificence was such, however, that he followed his first gift with a further twenty-eight acres after only a few months for the extra provision of football and cricket pitches and tennis courts. As a result, he was made the first Honorary Freeman of the Borough, and it was then that the subscription lists for a statue were opened. Four thousand people contributed. The statue was erected in 1891 at the east end of Broad Street, but it was moved to Palmer's Park in 1928 in view of what was then considered a traffic problem. The sculptor was a local man, George Simmonds, who was said to have shown Palmer's slightly stooping posture and large family nose 'more truly than any portrait'.

Sir Henry Waterlow, who went to stand in Waterlow Park, Highgate in 1900, was the son of a printer. He joined his father's business in Birchin Lane in the City in 1844, bought Lauderdale House, which stands in what is now Waterlow Park, in 1865, but never lived there. He was Lord Mayor of London from 1872/3. In 1899 he gave the Park to the London County Council 'to provide a garden for the gardenless.' The statue, by F.M. Taubman, erected six years before he died, is in a spot with a commanding view over the Highgate Cemetery which in turn is dominated by the armless and umbrellarly impotent Karl Marx.

Nine

GALLANT

HAD Mrs Worthington asked Douglas Jerrold's father for advice, it would have been very different from that which she received from Noel Coward. Jerrold senior was *most* anxious to put his son on the stage, but young Douglas would have none of it. He did write for the theatre but it is as a journalist that he is best remembered. Quick to champion causes of injustice, he nevertheless didn't worry about upsetting friend or foe with his acerbic wit.

'He was so benevolent, so merciful a man that he would have held an umbrella over a duck in a shower of rain' might therefore have been either cynicism or flattery. Was 'he' just a silly old man – for surely it would have been lovely weather for ducks – or a man like Mr Paice 'tenderly escorting a market woman, whom he had encountered in a shower, exalting his umbrella over her basket of fruit, that it might receive no damage, with as much carefulness as if she had been a countess.'? Joseph Paice 'was the only pattern of consistent gallantry' Charles Lamb had met, though Paice was 'bred a Presbyterian and brought up a merchant'.

Charles Lamb called it gallantry, but was it? Is there not a distinction between gallantry and manners? Surely it was not gallantry that 'Captain Brown shook hands with no one until he had helped Miss Brown to unfurl her umbrella.' Gallantry is not practised among relations or between members of the same sex. Does it not imply some hope of sexual favour in return? Was it only the weather that Captain Wentworth had in mind when he 'equipped himself properly for Bath'? The day after he arrived, he was able to ask Anne Elliot to make use of the new umbrella if she were determined to walk.

Maybe Captain Wentworth and Psmith were demi-gallants. Unrelated to the subjects of their attentions on first encounter but in pursuance, considerate but calculating. Did they have something in common with Daisy Ashford's

character in *The Young Visitors*? 'I am not quite a gentleman, but you would hardly notice it.'

Totally gallant was the Downland shepherd.

Before the First World War, it was common practice for shepherds to have large green umbrellas with ribs of cane or whalebone. On fine days, they would sling the cord attached to the ferrule across their backs to carry them. On wet days, they pushed the umbrellas well back into the bushes to get such protection from wind and rain as they could. Barclay Wills recorded the tale of the shepherd who called his umbrella 'the big 'un' and recollected how, having met up with shepherds from outlying farms for a chat, they happened to get caught in a sudden shower.

'Not far from where they stood, a man and a maid were sitting on a bank, and one of the shepherds suggested that my friend should take his umbrella and share it with the couple. On the spur of the moment he accepted the challenge and walked across to them with the big umbrella open. To his amazement, the girl's companion rose and ran away as fast as he could, leaving her on the bank. He evidently suspected with the young shepherd's advance and the merriment of the others that some plot was afoot, and, like the coward he was, left the girl to her fate. It would seem that he had no particular claim to her affections and that she was inclined to appreciate the young shepherd's action, for she sat quite still and allowed him to shelter her from the rain in gallant fashion. "I diddun' mine they chaps grinnin", he told me, "fur she were a pretty gil, an' tarked to I. 'Doannt 'ee put t'umbrella down,' she says when t'rain stopped. 'Kip 'um up a bit, fur I likes being 'ere 'long o you.' But I *did* put 'un down, for t'dig telled I to." The old shepherd chuckled and rubbed his head. "Damme, I'd nigh forgot 'bout it all," he said, "till you comed tarkin' 'bout they umbrellas."'

Ten

CHARACTERISTIC

N O ONE will argue much over the fact that owner and dog grow to look alike. So too with umbrellas, which 'like faces, acquire a certain sympathy with the individual who carries them.'

Sarah Gamp's umbrella had a will of its own with its 'independent malice' and she had so little control of it that she was party to its caprice. Take the moment when the hooked handle catches Tom Pinch around the throat. Disengaging himself, with perfect good humour, he then gets the ferrule in his back and the hook round his ankle. Gamp then flops around his head like a great bird before he gets a thrust in the ribs, suffering 'exceeding anguish'. There was nothing Sarah could do about it.

Citizen King, Louis Philippe, was an oddity among French monarchs. A man with a happy marriage; a man of unselfish cast. But, poor soul, he was pear-shaped and he carried an umbrella. It was all so bourgeois, and a gift to cartoonist and critic who saw Louis under a 'vast sentimental umbrella' offering the French 'the illusion of being free, prosperous and glorious'. It was suggested that had he been able to 'substitute an umbrella for a sceptre' he would have been happier.

Father Brown, the very embodiment of all that's homely and helpless 'shambled into the room a shapeless little figure which seemed to find its own hat and umbrella as unmanageable as a mass of luggage . . . the umbrella black . . . the prosaic handle long past repair.'

There was a difference of opinion between Spider McCoy and his orphan niece Margie as to whether Jonas, hardly named by accident, was or was not 'a big umbrella'. Fight manager Spider had seen Jonas flatten the non-paying passenger of a taxi, although Jonas was later to explain that he 'just put out my right hand to ward him off, and he runs into it with his chin and knocks himself unconscious.' Nevertheless, Spider still saw Jonas, as he had seen many others in the past, as 'the next heavyweight champion of the world'.

'Good grief', Margie says, 'another big umbrella.'
'What do you mean, umbrella?' Spider says.
'Why', Margie says, 'something that folds up.'

Jonas turned out to be a 'once king' who got 'the old hoovus-groovus from a dictator'. Margie thought 'there must be anyway a trace of umbrella in a character who lets anybody run him out of his own country.'

Spider found it a disappointment that Jonas refused to go into the ring wearing either a crown or a monocle, but nevertheless he was pretty good at 'tank jobs' until he was 'slightly bewildered the night at the Sun Casino when a generally reliable waterboy misses his cue and falls down before Jonas can hit him.'

Jonas saw an approach to return home to discuss being king again as 'at least a chance to pick up a few belongings that he didn't have time to collect the last time he departed.' Once there, Dictator Pottafuss offered the throne in exchange for marriage to his moustached sister Sophia. The fright on Jonas's face got Spider thinking that maybe Margie

was right after all. 'He is a big umbrella.' But, in the ensuing brawl, Spider came into his own as fight manager. Pottapuss was flattened. Triumphant Jonas got Margie, leaving Spider to marry Sophia.

'It's no use, Margie,' said Spider, 'you are right, he is an umbrella;' but then it was Margie who was to disagree.

Eleven

UNISEX

NEITHER the umbrella nor the parasol gained quick acceptance in America, maybe because the Chinese didn't arrive on the Eastern seaboard until some time after the Europeans. Sidney Fisher's *Men, Women and Manners of Colonial Days*, published in 1898, recorded sightings in Philadelphia in 1771, but as a means of keeping off the sun they were regarded by the *Gazette* as a 'ridiculous effeminacy'. Only physicians saw merit – for warding off 'vertigoes, epilepsy, sore eyes, fevers, etc.'.

Frances Caulkins, writing a *History of Norwich* (New England) in 1866, reported that 'parasols and umbrellas were unknown or of a rare occurrence.' Instead of parasols 'women of mature age' used fans 'nearly a foot-and-a-half in length and spreading like the train of a peacock.' No alternative protection against the rain is mentioned.

By the late 1950s all that had changed. The Americans were not only into umbrellas in a big way, they didn't care much what they looked like. On his first visit to the States, Christopher Sykes said that 'umbrellas are looked upon by Americans simply as machines to keep off the rain, and their size and ornamentation in so far as it has no utilitarian purpose, is considered quite irrelevant.' Unisex had been invented. 'It is true that I do not remember seeing a female American using a large masculine Brigg-style umbrella but I very often saw, in fact more often than not, men of obviously well-to-do environment, upper-crust types without question, using or carrying dainty little feminine umbrellas. Much observation led me to the conclusion that in the United States umbrellas are not regarded as objects in any way related to sex.'

The English had had a go at unisex as far back as 1914 with the Cunliffe Shooting Seat which could be adapted to an umbrella for rainy days on the moors. It was sold 'for both men and women' by Mappin and Webb for 33s 6d.

Then along with the war came *La Militaire*, a straight-handled brolly which got its name from being carried underarm like a military baton. Once war-born utility was over, *The Bag, Portmanteau and Umbrella Trader* condemned it. *La Militaire* was 'so universally used by both men and women that people were just a little tired of it.'

Not surprisingly it is the French who solved the sex problem of the umbrella. They devised the double umbrella. From one handle, around which loving fingers may intertwine, two shafts emerge with an angle of some sixty degrees between them. Ribs radiate from the top of each, but the cover is cunningly joined to form one shade. Closed, with ferrules aloft, the brolly looks like a mini version of the twin spires of a Romantic cathedral.

In 1881 the Penelope Sun Umbrella Cover was marketed for converting umbrellas into sunshades. Washable covers came in white or cream satin, with various coloured bindings, and in four sizes.

A large slouched beaver umbrella that wanted only a crape hatband to sanctify it for a funeral.

C.L. LEWIS
Memoirs (1800)

Tax umbrellas, and make the Bishops order the prayers for rain to be read in all the churches till the end of the month.

WILLIAM PITT

Large red umbrellas were attached to buses owned by the Metropolitan Railway in the 1880s to shelter the drivers.

I spent a great deal of time and pains to make me an umbrella.

DANIEL DEFOE
Robinson Crusoe

Twelve

MUSICAL

I T'S ODD that nobody has ever thought of *playing* the umbrella. All it needs is a few Pan-like holes at appropriate intervals in the stick. The player would then pull and push the shuttle up and down just as the trumpeter might. The truly ingenious could use the cover for substitute bellows, thus making substantial savings on the amount of puff needed for more complicated instruments such as the bagpipes. The umbrella flute would, moreover, be of great advantage to the street musician with the built-in benefit of precipitate cover.

Even if one didn't play the actual umbrella, there are instruments to which it could well be attached as an accessory in its own right. Take, for example, the tuba. Invert it and it looks much like an umbrella with an overcomplicated handle. The right way up, just think how much rain the tuba could collect on a wet day. It's all very well being tuba player in the back row on the concert platform, but what does the rain do to the tone of the Salvation Army band outside the pub on Sunday? That's not the sort of problem Sousa had in mind though when he said, 'America doesn't want sadness; that's why I put sunshine into my music. Come to think of it, I'm an anti-umbrella man myself.'

In the theatre too the umbrella is much underused. Admittedly, there is danger in too sweeping a statement since productions vary so. Who would have thought of the Mafia getting their hands on *Rigoletto* before Jonathan Miller? In stage performances of *La Traviata* it is not unusual to see Germont carrying an umbrella; it is after all in keeping with the respectability of his nature. In the film version it is Alfredo who could have done with one in a most practical way.

Think for one moment what a useful prop an umbrella could be, particularly bearing in mind the frequency with which it is forgotten by its owner. Take the 'exit' aria, which

gives the opera singer an illogical chance to show off while contributing nothing to the plot. When *Scipione Africano* was first produced in 1664, it ended with the hero jumping off a burning boat and swimming away. Fourteen years later, he stopped for a final solo. He would hardly have been likely to go back for his umbrella on such an occasion 'tis true, but surely the forgotten brolly could have played a far greater part in, say, *opera buffa*, than it did. It certainly seems a more plausible reason for getting people back on stage than 'Anyone for tennis?' is for getting them off. Rossini appreciated the possibilities in that ridiculous excess of courteous exchanges when Don Basilio returns to retrieve his brolly in *The Barber of Seville*, but that doyen of librettists Carlo Goldoni, who had the wit to write under so many pseudonyms, all of which were near-anagrams of his name and included such inventions as Aldimiro Clog, never used an umbrella in his *cicisbeo* comedies of Venetian intrigue, either to complicate still further the action or indeed to suggest the sonority with which the very word *ombrellino* might have rolled up from the vocal chords.

Lighter music has had a few brollies. A man named Davidson produced a songbook of *Umbrella Courtship* in 1840; sadly, only its title seems to have survived. Bud Flanagan went on for years looking for umbrellas to mend. But the oddest umbrella song of all must have been the one written for a general election. In 1885, Lord Salisbury had claimed that 'We are all content to stand under Mr Gladstone's umbrella.' That's how *'Under the Umbrella'* came to be written as party propaganda.

Ballet must be one of the few arts which can come about when its two principal originators, composer and choreographer, never meet. A great number of years can separate the two, as umbrella ballets show.

The first performance of *La Fille mal Gardée* took place in Bordeaux in 1789 under the title *Ballet de la Paille*. It was revived at the Paris Opera in 1828 with new music by Hérold with a little help from Donizetti. Hertel wrote yet new music for it in 1864 and that was generally used until Ashton returned to Hérold in 1960. Actually it is a sad story for the protagonist of the umbrella, for Alain's brolly symbolizes his rustic simplicity. It is an impediment to his proposal in Act I, a reverse parachute carrying him up to the heavens in the thunderstorm at the end of Act II, and a comfort to him when he creeps back in the confusion of his rejection at the end.

Mayerling opens in Heilingenkreuz cemetery before dawn – with obvious high potential for the funereal umbrella. Act I does then open on celebrations in a Viennese ballroom, but in keeping with the decadence of the Empire at the time, the action goes back to the cemetery for the epilogue. The music incidentally was by Liszt – and the first Covent Garden production with choreography by MacMillan didn't happen until 1978.

Liszt can't have had all that in mind any more than Chopin could have imagined all those sylphs prancing around when he wrote his 'Nocturne' in A flat, Op. 32, No. 2. The classical ballet skirt made its debut with *Sylphides*, but the tutu which sticks out rather like a Ben Jonson umbrella around a higher part of the anatomy is in fact a slang term referring to that which it no longer covers. A *Sylphide* parasol was illustrated in *La Gazette des Salons* in 1839. It had a frilly skirt hanging from eliptically scalloped edges.

Chopin's music was also used for a one-act ballet which Robbins choreographed in 1956. Its subtitle is *The Perils of Everybody* and it had its brollies.

Dances with integral brollies are also known outside the theatre, both in Hungary and in Belgium where there is a special *cotillion* known as *La Parapluiterie*. Such dances are peasant- and passion-orientated, but there's drama in India with the *Kudaikutti*, which, although known more familiarly as the 'Umbrella Dance', is all about the god of war killing demons.

Dancing in frustration are the brollies seen on a wet day in our own big cities. Go down any alley-way, or better still look for the sign 'Messrs So and So regret any inconvenience to the public', for there, like as not, you will find scaffolding and access to the pavement severely restricted. When umbrella meets umbrella, one pops up; one down. One skips to the left; one to the right. *Chassé, épaulement* even; *pirouette, glissade*. And if it's very crowded, *sissone*, or, indeed, *arabesque* if the gentleman has to stand on one leg, lean out and clutch the scaffolding if he is to retain his balance while the lady passes. A veritable *ballon* of brollies. All to the sounds of the busy city – the fire engine, the klaxon, the *perpetuum mobile* of the erratic burglar alarm, the silencer that isn't. The conductor is the common time of the traffic lights. The music of the metropolis; the ballet of the brollies.

✶ **Asking for sausages at the florist's shop or opening his umbrella on a sunny day were ways of relaxing the imagination and inducing the bizarre.**

Obituary of Philippe Souppault (March 1990)

✶ **Georgi Markov was murdered with a poisoned umbrella at a bus stop on Waterloo Bridge in 1978.**

✶ **I unwillingly donned a cloak, and took my umbrella to accompany her on a stroll to the bottom of the park; a formal walk which she generally affected if low-spirited.**

EMILY BRONTË

✶ **Stout cherry handle and serviceable alpaca; marks at a glance the decorous hard-working parson.**

Advertisement for a clerical umbrella (1873)

✶ ***The Lady's Pictorial*** **of 1887 noted an umbrella with a watch built into the handle 'so that one can time a call exactly.'**

Thirteen

ARTISTIC

THE first-known English drawing of an umbrella dates from the end of the tenth century when monks at Canterbury produced their own version of the Utrecht Psalter, which by that time may have been anything up to three hundred years old. In the original, David is leaping from the top of a cloud into a temple while a heavily-winged angel stands behind with a small open umbrella. The monks removed the wings from the angel and increased the size of the brolly, although they lacked the foresight of harnessing it like a parachute to David to ensure safe transit.

English art is then pretty bereft of brollies for eight hundred years or so. There is the famous Elizabethan painting of Sir Henry Unton on his journey from Oxford to Padua in which he has a white parasol to shade him from the sun, but art of the true umbrella would appear to date only from eighteenth-century caricaturists such as Gillray and Cruickshank. The difficulties of putting up and coping with umbrellas provided endless opportunities. One of Cruickshank's most famous is entitled *Eccentricities and Monstrosities*. Gillray's *A Modern Belle Going to the Rooms at Bath* is splendid social history. The lady is being transported in a sedan chair. Her head-dress is so elaborate that the roof of the chair is open to allow her fine ostrich feather plumes to protrude uncrumpled. The bearer at the back has a brolly with parabolic handle so that the cover reaches over to protect the exposed feathers. Jonas was just ten years dead when it appeared, sedan chair carriers were still protesting that the brolly was threatening their livelihood and Bath was full of Captain Wentworths.

The first 'serious' umbrella artist may well have been Joseph Wright, who in 1782 painted the Revd D'Ewes Cole and his wife Hannah together with Daniel Parker Coke MP. It is an outdoor scene. Mr Parker Coke is seated at a table whereon lies an umbrella. The reverend gentleman is

pointing across the valley. Were it the twentieth century, one would suspect him of lobbying for planning permission.

Our most prolific umbrella artist was another humourist, Heath Robinson. The uses he saw for umbrellas included keeping Guy Fawkes bonfires going under difficulties, masking bashed headlamps on early motor cars, and shielding wasp guns. He is probably best remembered for his *Railway Ribaldry*, which has a multiplicity of brollies. ('A railway is not merely a matter of railway trains but of stations, signals, waiting-rooms, booking and lost property offices, tunnels and no end of other things as well.') In *Old Gentleman Recognising his lost Umbrella in the Brolly Department of the Lost Property Office*, the brollies go round on wires rather as little cash drums used to do in old department stores in the days before we paid for everything with plastic. Heath Robinson also put brollies on top of signals, frequently to protect a nesting bird, on engines to keep the funnels dry, and at all sorts of places along the track.

Transport features in serious umbrella art too. There's that depressing picture by Ford Madox Brown, *The Last of England*, painted between 1852 and 1855 when nineteenth-century emigration was at its height. Brown had considered it. Using himself and his wife as models, he explained, 'I have in order to present the parting scene in its fullest tragic development, singled out a couple from the middle classes, high enough through education and refinement to appreciate all that they are now giving up . . . The husband broods bitterly over blighted hopes and severance from all that he has been striving for.' He also looks as though he is about to be seasick.

Discomfort also seems to be the trouble for Rossiter's people going to *Brighton and Back for 3/6d*, painted in 1859, as they travelled in an open-sided wagon. One passenger is trying hard to fend off the elements with his umbrella. Joy's *Bayswater Omnibus* of 1895, however, has all the elegance of a silk-hatted gentleman, quite removed from the man on the Clapham omnibus, and a fashionable lady with folded brolly by her side.

On the whole, the Victorians were romantics, and the prettiness of the parasol is much more in evidence in their art than the utilitarian brolly. Were they trying to forget their dark satanic mills – or just the weather? Horsley's *Showing a Preference* in 1860 has the suitor preferring the lady with the parasol to the lady without. Both ladies have parasols in Mulready's *Good Natured Cousins*, and Wilkinson shades both flowers and seller in his *Spring in Piccadilly* of 1887. *The Lady Returning from Confirmation* with sailor-suited suppliant in Hallyar's painting of 1888 naturally carries a pure pastel parasol.

It took a couple of Frenchmen to get to grips with the brolly.

Renoir probably started on *Les Parapluies* in the early 1880s, painting first the right-hand side and returning to complete the picture some years later after travelling in Algeria and Italy. In the early 1880s, Renoir was in what he himself called his 'sour period'. Writing to Vollard he said, 'I wanted to tell you that in about 1883 there occurred a kind of break in my work. I had got to the end of Impressionism and I had come to the conclusion that I didn't know either how to paint or how to draw. In short, I had come to a dead end.' Critics may say that *Les Parapluies* is by no means one of his best works – it is said to lack 'spontaneity in the interest of decorative gain' – and Pissarro said of Renoir's work at the time that 'without the lovely colours he used to use so instinctively, he is incoherent.' Nevertheless, many of us still like going to look at it in the National Gallery and derive great pleasure from doing so.

Then there was Tissot. Born to parents in the clothing business, he developed an abiding interest in fashion, and was something of a dandy himself. He didn't come to London until 1872, after the fall of the *Commune*, which he had supported, but he had already contributed a number of caricatures to *Vanity Fair*. This he continued to do. There is one of George John Whyte-Melville whom *Vanity Fair* called a 'novelist of Society' who wrote of 'modern life of the better kind'. Whyte-Melville is pictured posed on a buttoned-velvet couch, wearing a top hat and a drooping moustache matched to a drooping tie. The elegantly slim umbrella, held prominently by the left hand, points ferrule to elegant footwear.

But even Tissot succumbed to Victorian parasol fever. The theme of *Portsmouth Dockyard* (now in the Tate) is the same as Horsley's – a sort of 'how happy could I be with either.' Tissot's setting is however a rowing boat which appears to be heading straight for the bows of some huge sea-going vessel. Tissot was very fond of painting boats, although they never seemed to get outside the harbour walls.

Perhaps he suffered from *mal de mer*. Seated between a pair of pretty young ladies in the little boat is a Highland soldier, wearing a bonnet far larger than either of the ladies and displaying a great deal of bare leg. The ladies' elegant ruffled dresses naturally hide all. Surely they must be parasols that the ladies carry – one up, one down – for they would hardly have gone boating in the rain. Yet the sky looks ominous, and there is no sign of shadow to suggest it was other than the dullest of days. The gentleman appears to favour the more optimistic of the two ladies whose parasol/umbrella/what-have-you is closed, although the original title of the picture was *Between the Two My Heart is Balanced*. Obviously he was in a boat he had no intention of rocking. It took nearly another seventy years for one of Chagall's cows to show what a jolly thing a parasol could really be.

Tissot returned to Paris in 1882 and set about a series of paintings known as *Women in Paris*. One of these is *The Bridesmaid*, which later found its way back to Leeds Art Gallery. There is no doubt this time that he was into umbrellas proper. The bridesmaid, dressed in bustled blue silk with matching flowers on her bonnet, is being helped into a carriage by a large gentleman holding an even larger umbrella over her. Grey-clad, umbrellaless workers of both sexes look on, but in the busy-ness of the pedestrian background, two more grey brollies can just be seen.

In the twentieth century, the utilitarian aspect of the umbrella has had a more established place in English art. Perhaps it is all to do with a greater acceptance of reality, and knowing the unpleasantness of much that is real. Nevinson, a great military painter in the First World War, who was to call for art to be 'strong, virile and unsentimental', gave us a rain-soaked London in his *Oxford Street* of 1919. Sickert, who later in his life painted quite frequently from news photos, recorded *Miss Erhart's Arrival* as the first woman to fly solo across the Atlantic in 1932. It was a very wet day.

Foreigners saw the umbrella as a symbol of all that is English and painted it too. In 1938, Chiang Lee published *The Silent Traveller in London* and among the illustrations is his *Umbrellas under Big Ben*. 'I could not see the faces, but only the movement of umbrellas.' For a Chinaman it can hardly have been a strange sight.

During the Second World War, David Langdon's bowler-hatted Billy Brown always had his umbrella under his arm in the propaganda posters up and down the escalators. Linked again to transport was William Robert's *Rush Hour* in the late Fifties. Depicting the struggle to get on a bus to Waterloo, it also showed just how easy it is to lose an umbrella even before one gets on a train.

Then along came that story-teller of painters, Helen Bradley. Discouraged when young, for her father told her 'there's nothing in art for a woman – you stick to embroidery instead', it wasn't until the mid-Sixties that she started to relive in her art the memories of her Lancashire childhood. Umbrellas abounded. There's hardly a character without one on Blackpool station for example. And the number propped against luggage suggests anticipation of the need for that oh-so-English piece of equipment for a holiday by the English sea.

🌴 The men in the audience struck at her with fists and umbrellas as she was carried past them. Asquith stood silent with contracted lips.

SYLVIA PANKHURST

🌴 Abraham Lincoln travelled with 'nothing more than he could carry in his saddlebag and his cotton umbrella.'

🌴 Shut up, an umbrella is an unmanageable walking stick; open, it is an inadequate tent.

G.K. CHESTERTON

🌴 ... trees clipped low till they spread out into umbrellas.

ELIZABETH BOWEN

🌴 ... our American partner and ultimate umbrella

SIR CLIFFORD MILES
at a Seminar on Nuclear Shelters, October 1980

🌴 The chattels of Mrs Bloss were forwarded by instalments. First there came a large hamper of Guinness's Stout and an umbrella.

CHARLES DICKENS

🌴 ... a bastard born out of a walking stick and a cabriolet.

HONORÉ DE BALZAC

🌴 The umbrella skirt was high fashion in the early 1890s. Cut on the cross from material double normal width, one seam, worn at the back, was concealed under box pleats which fell to the ground in a small train.

Fourteen

SCULPTURAL

C OMTE de Lautréamont was the pseudonym of Isidore-Lucien Ducasse, a writer of little reputation until the Surrealists resurrected him some sixty years after his death. The *Comte* had defined beauty as 'the chance meeting of a sewing-machine and an umbrella on the dissecting table', and this was just what they needed to justify the medium of *objets trouvés* (garbage to the man in the street) used in exhibits at their International Surrealist Exhibition in 1936.

Any *parapluies trouvées'd* among the *objets* are no doubt by now *perdues*.

More durable is the work of Henry Moore. He was not only much concerned with his reputation but with the precise placing and preservation of his output. In later life he arrived to stay with friends in Switzerland who had collected a number of his larger pieces. They were disturbed as to how they could possibly entertain him when the weather was so appallingly wet. Moore was quick to put their apprehensions aside. On arrival, he announced, 'You are no doubt worried what to do with me all weekend, but don't worry, I shall just look at my sculpture', which he apparently did, trudging round the rain-sodden garden under a large umbrella, though it was surely more in self-interest than any gallant attempt to protect any reclining woman from the wrath of nature.

Andrew Carnie built a sculpture from brollies in the early 1980s and protected it with the built-in. Two figures are going for a walk; brolly legs, brolly bodies, brolly arms, one of each pair holding a brolly aloft. With brolly held ferrule in hand, the handle latches on to the collar of a bent-brolly dog.

Carnie may have produced a rather charming terrestial pair, walking the dog on Sunday afternoon, but scientists now sculpt for space. Lockheed's space antennae look much like a domestic umbrella except that the ribs are above the cover rather than underneath. In embryonic form each rib is rolled up like a tape measure. Once into space the ribs spring open to hold a brolly which can then be used for radio experimentation. It is 180 ft in diameter.

If the hidden persuaders had their way we would all have little umbrella sculptures in our gardens to bring satellite messages down into our living rooms. Dubbed 'unsightly bird-baths' by villagers who tried to ban them and ranking high among items raising *angst* among neighbours, there is at last a transparent and inevitably 'environmentally friendly' dish which needs only the window-cleaner to spruce it up from time to time. All the Chinese have to do of course is tilt their coolie-hatted heads backwards. A case of *plus ça change*, if they have a head-start on us yet again.

On the train to Shanghai, Michael Palin asked the Chinese girl, 'What is the one question you would like to ask an Englishman?' She replied, 'Do you carry an umbrella?'

I can't tell you its name, but I can tell you its history. Strangers take it away.

RALPH WALDO EMERSON

Jo showed how happy she would be to walk through life beside him, even though she had no better shelter than the old umbrella if he carried it.

LOUISA M. ALCOTT
Good Wives

Umbrellas with their feathers
Shield you in all sorts of weathers.

MICHAEL DRAYTON

'Umbrellas are just not an aerodynamic shape,' concluded Dr Garry of the College of Aeronautics after wind-tunnel tests showed none coped with a windspeed greater than 32 mph. Some blew inside out at only 10.

. . . a magnificent family red silk umbrella . . . the little boys mobbed it and called it a stick in petticoats.

MRS GASKELL
Cranford

Cazal, umbrella-maker to Louis-Philippe's wife, survived the 1848 revolution to carry on as umbrella-maker to the Empress Eugénie.

Robert Louis Stevenson gave his umbrella to Rudyard Kipling as a mark of respect and affection.

Fifteen

ARCHITECTURAL

M R Batty Langley published *Ancient Architecture Restored* in 1742. Batty was his real name; it would have been unthinkable for a man who specialized in 'Nobleman's Seats . . . executed in the most grand taste . . . Pavilions and other Rural Buildings of Pleasure', etc. ever to be given such a nickname.

Among his designs was the umbrella roof for open-sided arbours, sometimes of wood but more often of stone, placed at the end of garden walks. The idea was not new. The ancient Athenians had had umbrella roofs, and many will have seen the Temple di Bacio in the gardens of the Villa Cimbrone at Ravello in southern Italy.

Odd that it should be an *umbrella* roof – for one was hardly likely to sit in an arbour in a rainstorm, although one cannot know either the state of Wagner's mind nor his habits when it came to his writing *Parsifal* while staying at the Cimbrone.

The English, though, had a funny habit in the eighteenth century. If they felt things were a little inferior they tended to use foreign words to describe them. If they felt their park was a little less grand than that of the neighbours, they called it a *jardin anglais*.

Whatever he called his park, the second earl at Castle Howard had a folly which was known as an '*Umbrello*' in his Menagerie Wood. It was built to a specification similar to one at Strawberry Hill, but now it is nought but a pile of rubble.

Other '*umbrellos*' were less grand. Covers could be of wood, tin, or even canvas, but the seats underneath would always be circular, thus determining the umbrella shape of the roof.

Stourhead used to have a very grand umbrella. It was crowned by a pineapple and supported by Doric columns. A drawing was made of it in 1779 by a Mr Piper, but, together with a Gothick Greenhouse and a Turkish Tent, it was pulled down by Sir Richard Hoare, whose reputation, other

than as a banker, was to rest on the fact that it was he who first planted the rhododendrons.

Sir William Chambers built the 163 ft-high pagoda at Kew with ten umbrellas on top of each other in 1761.

On much smaller scale and much later came that strange little house, Umbrella Cottage, in Dorset. Oak pillars with carved owls support a thatched roof which curves down to elliptical edges to resemble an open umbrella.

Semi-umbrella houses were spotted by G.K. Chesterton as he travelled out through the suburbs of north London in the 1930s. They had 'porches capped with those quaint sort of cupolas like wooden umbrellas that one sees in some old-fashioned houses.' Of their time, he considered the houses 'very English and very suburban in the good old wealthy Clapham sense.'

Following the march of tourism, the umbrella took a step back out into the garden. It needed no foreign name, for origin said all. 'I leant back in my gaily coloured deckchair, observing contentedly the sparrows disporting in the bird-bath against the lawn, under the well-creosoted trellis with the ramblers. Butch, our miniature poodle, lay newly clipped at my feet. Above my head spread the striped beach umbrella we had brought back from Fuengirola, stuck in its flowerpot of gravel. It was a glorious summer evening, the sun still high over the conical yew, the patio glowing in the nook beside the car port. We were sipping our gin-and-Slimlines, while the wife in the kitchen was preparing our dinner and listening to the Archers.' The totality of suburbia as seen by Richard Gordon.

Sixteen

VERBAL

T HE pace of change in a living language accelerates as means of communication through both travel and media quicken. Pedants today may pride themselves then that 'our word', although only some four hundred years old, has been remarkably stable. Firm in its Latin root *umbra*, it did however first mean a sunshade; it wasn't until the mid-seventeenth century that it acquired its wet connotations.

Sobriquets are in a class of their own. The French, way ahead of the English in having umbrellas at all, were also first with a nickname, the 'Pepin'. Pepin the Short, as he was known, was a king from around the Schleswig-Holstein area who was given a jewel-handled umbrella by Pope Paul I in part settlement of a dispute over lands. Some centuries later, the French were carrying 'Robinsons'. Mr Crusoe was translated over there and became immensely popular. The term still endures.

The English flirted for a little while with their 'Hanways', but took their first real sobriquet from the French. 'Gingham' crept into the language in the early 1860s. Some say it is derived from the Malay, but more believe it is a mispronunciation of Guingamp, a small town in Brittany where gingham as we call it was dyed and made into umbrella covers before the introduction of silk. Calverley uses the term in the last verse of his lament for 'The New Hat' ruined in a storm.

> How I lov'd thee, my Bright One! I pluck in remorse
> My hands from my pockets and wring 'em:
> Oh, why did not I, dear, as a matter of course,
> Ere I purchased thee purchase a gingham.

Sarah 'Gamp' came along in 1864.

'Brolly' lives on too. Since an umbrella can be an accessory of some dignity, the Earl of Chesterfield might have been quite disturbed had he known that 'brolly' originated from Winchester. 'Words are the dress of thoughts, which should no more be presented in rags, tatters and dirt, than your person should', said he. 'Brolly', not recognized by the *Oxford English Dictionary* until 1874, is to be found in an 1842 manuscript word book in the school's collection and in an 1866 publication *School Life at Winchester College* by R.B. Mansfield who was a scholar there from 1836–42. Wykehamists had a special language, 'Notions'; with 'tolly' for candle, 'yolly' for yellow, etc., one can understand how the 'brolly' came to be. The scholars took their new language with them to the old universities, whence it spread, with them, to the Empire.

In the twentieth century, our *Chamberlains* turned out to be scarcely less ephemeral than a piece of paper.

Umbrella slang arrived in Victorian days, first with 'umbrella' used for a broad-rimmed hat. In the 1880s 'he has a regular umbrella' signified disdain for long, thick hair: Victorian teddy-boys, in other words. People who needed to be 'measured for a new umbrella' were badly dressed, and he of whom it was said 'only his umbrella fits' was stupid.

'Brolly hopping' got into the language in 1934 when a *Daily Express* reporter used it in connection with parachute jumps made by the RAF. 'Umbrella' became synonymous with parachute and the 'umbrella man' was he who dropped.

Today, the 'umbrella brigade' is the Special Branch of the British police force.

Slang is often thought of as something we import from America. Lease-lend in language is a two-way business though, and the American today might say that he had forgotten his 'bumbershoot' or his 'mush'. A mush-faker was a Victorian umbrella repairer.

There is still one place in the world where the umbrella speaks sentences if not volumes, and that is Asante. Speech there is paralipsical; the speaker omits to mention the very thing to which he wishes to refer. In the 1880s, an Asante chief called on British Governor Rowe. The chief said, 'I have come down to stop all these small leaks in the roof which have been giving us trouble of late. If I cannot do this, we must have a new roof.' What he meant was, 'I come to seek peace.' The English, who had never had much of a reputation for languages, knew a lot about diplomacy. Governor Rowe replied, 'I am not a mudfish.' The Asante chief knew that Rowe meant that he was a good sort of chap and prepared to negotiate.

The linguistic connection with umbrellas may at first seem a little far-fetched, but it is not just that the Asante have very large umbrellas, they translate the proverbs of their everyday speech into images which they put on top of them. As late as 1940, a splendid example was found in Kumasi. It was a wooden hen and a whole brood of chicks. The literal meaning was 'a hen may step on her chicks but never so heavily as to kill them', and the figurative, 'punishment or misfortune must always be mixed with mercy.' That little topping to the brolly is $2\frac{1}{2}$ ft high. An even bigger one, nearly 4 ft high, probably made in the 1920s, shows a snake biting a hornbill. Even though a snake can't fly, it will catch the hornbill if the bird owes it money.

Although it may seem that everything can be explained once you know what you're talking about, the British persisted in taking away the best of umbrellas. Baden-Powell not only captured that of King Koffee Kakalli in 1874, but went on to acquire King Prempeh I's a year later even though 'the drums of Kumasi talked peace'. Baden-Powell apparently acquired Prempeh's hat, but his favourite umbrella was dispatched to a museum in South Kensington. It is now in the Museum of Mankind. Prempeh himself was exiled to the Seychelles but eventually allowed to return home where he lived on to become president of the local Boy Scouts Association!

Seventeen

MARTIAL

URLED, the umbrella cannot fulfil its real and perhaps immediate purpose. Any offensive movement is more likely to be a *coup de curiosité* than a *coup de grâce*. The rambler prods the toadstool, just in case it can be fried with the morning's breakfast. The old gentleman, sitting idly on the park bench, spears the wind-swept paper teasing his feet.

Open, the umbrella is a weapon of defence.

In 1758 Dr Shebbare had the wit to ask for one when sentenced to a day in the stocks.

Intrepid travellers were advised that 'a parasol will put to flight the most persistent tiger if opened smartly in its face.'

The sheriff of Middlesex who granted Dr Shebbare's request was himself subsequently tried for 'excessive leniency', but the idea that the umbrella dispelled animals was perpetuated when George Borrow wrote, 'What need he fear if a wild bull or ferocious dog attacks him, provided he has a good umbrella. He unfurls the umbrella in the face of the bull or dog and the brute turns around quite scared and runs away.'

Ladies too have found the umbrella a useful defence. Mrs Emma Hardy set about an unduly familiar shoe-black in Rome in 1887. On a gentler note, Gwen Raverat tells how young ladies being punted up to Grantchester shielded their eyes from local youths plunging naked into the Cam.

But the brolly also has a place in true martial arts. Kings of Assyria led their armies into battle under umbrellas, but they were insignia – a thing of might and mystery – as well as useful in keeping off the sun. Princes of Siam had seven-tiered umbrellas for their elephant combat troops; their Burmese invaders only five. Camouflage was plainly yet to be invented, although if one were going to war on an elephant it probably wouldn't be of much use anyway.

Umbrellas didn't get mixed up with Western wars until much later. General Sir Thomas Picton was reported as riding to the battle of Vittoria not only in gentleman's dress of frock coat and top hat but carrying an umbrella. But it was raining at the time.

The Duke of Wellington comes next. 'His Grace, on looking round [at the Grenadier Guards advancing at Bayonne in 1813] saw, to his surprise, a great many umbrellas with which the officers protected themselves from the rain that was then falling,' reported Captain Gronow in his *Reminiscences and Recollections*. Arthur Hill was dispatched at the gallop to command 'Lord Wellington does not approve the use of umbrellas during the enemy's firing, and will not allow gentlemen's sons to make themselves ridiculous in the eyes of the army. . . . The Guards may in uniform, when on duty at St James's, carry them if they please, but in the field it is not only ridiculous but unmilitary.'

Cartoons appeared in French papers of English officers in Paris in 1814 on horseback, wearing scarlet uniforms, chimney pot hats and holding aloft bright green umbrellas. And, ridiculous they went on to be, for at Waterloo Marshal Soult described the English as not just ridiculous but 'eminently so'. 'It was raining and the English officers were on horseback, each with an umbrella in his hand.' It was nevertheless at the Charge of the Light Brigade in the Crimea, not Waterloo, that the French general Bosquet said, '*C'est magnifique, mais ce n'est pas la guerre.*' At Waterloo, Soult was merely surprised that 'all at once the English closed their umbrellas, hung them on their saddles, drew their sabres, and threw themselves upon our *Chausseurs.*'

A year later, Baron Lejeune, who was both an eminent French soldier and a talented painter of scenes from battles, said he had been amused to see English officers 'riding about in uniform holding parasols above their heads, [but] the fact that they use umbrellas and parasols, though it is not the fashion to do so in the French army, does not prevent them from being very brave soldiers in battle.'

By this time Wellington had given his name to the boot. Leather, above the knee to the fore but cut away behind, it was far from the pedestrian rubber of today. Hanging up his boots, Wellington went on to a long and distinguished career in politics and public life. As Prime Minister, living at No. 10, he found his brolly useful in a confrontation with his nephew Long-Wellesley over the custody of his children. With a sword at his, the Duke's, throat, His Grace calmly said,

'Wellesley, for thirty years I have faced the most practised killers in the world,' courage reinforced by his having to hand 'an umbrella from which a lethal blade could be sprung for purposes of self-defence against maniacs.' His Grace was taking greater precautions than Tweedledum, who, preparing for the rattle battle got himself into rather a mess, first trying to hide under his umbrella and then trying to fold it up while still inside. 'Such an extraordinary thing to do.' When Alice eventually helped to dress the pair, Tweedledum had the sword. 'Tweedledee, you can have the umbrella – it's quite as sharp.'

Wellington may not have been the greatest umbrella-carrier of all time, but he was probably the richest and certainly the most titled. He is said to have acquired more than a million pounds from his military exploits. His 'share' from the Waterloo prize money alone was £60,000, although he waived half of it. (Generals got £1,250, sergeants £9 and privates £2 10s.)

He enjoyed the title of Prince of Waterloo from gift by the King of the Netherlands of the estate at La Belle Alliance; he was Duke of Ciudad Rodrigo, of Bruney, and of Vittoria; Marquis of Duro, and of Torres Vedras; Count of Vimiera; Grandee of Spain (First Class); Marshal of Russia, Austria, France, Prussia, Portugal and the Netherlands; Captain General of Spain; and Knight of far too many things to mention other than the Garter, the Bath, the Golden Fleece and the Holy Ghost, the last being a kind of substitute award from Louis XVIII who had wanted to give him first the Château of Chambord and later Grosbois but, frustrated in his plans, could only offer the Holy Ghost set in diamonds. 'Such a man as Europe has not seen since Julius Caesar,' said Sir Walter Scott. But our last ducal Prime Minister aged as we all do, and latterly was said to carry the Sword of State, and no doubt his umbrella, at a 'regicidal angle of incidence'. But, protected by his boots below and by his brolly above, he kept them all waiting, for, as Brougham said, 'Westminster Abbey is yawning for him.'

Waterloo over, Britain enjoyed a good number of years without military conflict and the brolly became a truly pacific appendage even to the military themselves. The royal Commander-in-Chief, the Duke of Cambridge, was a renowned umbrella carrier, both in and out of uniform, and the chant which followed a somewhat wet review in the 1820s went:

> We don't want to fight,
> But by jingo if we do,
> We've got the Duke of Cambridge
> And his umbrella too.

Punch came along in 1845 suggesting that there should be a regiment called the First Parapluies and a cavalry corps the Heavy Gingham. It even published a battle song, somewhat cosmopolitan, which included lines such as: 'Wave high the stout umbrella', 'Unfurl, unfurl, the gingham', and 'wield the parapluie'. It ended, however, with acknowledgement of duality:

> The road to glory's plain
> Whene'er that *parapluie* appears
> Which p'raps will brave a thousand years
> The battle and the rain.

Then came the Crimean War. Lord Raglan, born Fitzroy James Henry Somerset and nephew of Wellington by marriage, was a veteran of the Peninsula. Wellington said that Raglan was a man who couldn't tell a lie to save his life, even though he persisted in referring to the Crimean enemy as 'the French'. *He* took an umbrella with him, and indeed is reported to have been rarely without it. Maybe he kept it up his sleeve. Strange how these military men have been responsible for so much of our wardrobe.

Later still, that very model for Gilbert's modern Major-General, Sir Garnet Wolseley, ordered ten thousand umbrellas for troops being sent to Egypt. It was his total commitment to practicality combined with style that led to the saying 'All Sir Garnet' to mean everything is going well in right and proper fashion. He did have his little eccentricities though and these included having an ornamental plaster cast made of his wife's dainty little foot. Too small no doubt to double as an umbrella stand.

The English were not alone in being 'ridiculous' in war. The King of Bavaria, who ruled from 1864 to 1886, wore a brolly with his general's uniform, but he was particularly proud of his fine head of hair. And the Chinese, with whom

it all started, lost the Battle of Ping Yang because they were too busy with their brollies trying to keep their powder dry.

The proud Prussians too saw the benefits, as Marie Stopes found on a visit to Berlin in 1903. 'No one but I laughed openly in the street on seeing a lady in a heavy rainstorm holding her umbrella over the head of a tall Prussian officer so as to protect him and his uniform while her thin silk dress was drenched. But I was severely reproved that my frivolous mind did not perceive that all the flourishes in a uniform should be preserved immaculate.'

Umbrellas still weren't totally accepted by British military men though, for in 1910 there is a story of a colonel of the 22nd Regiment on duty in Guernsey rushing from his club to break an offending umbrella over the head of one of his men so unfortunate as to be seen carrying one. Physically and spiritually bruised, the subaltern explained, 'Please, Sir, it's the General's.'

Umbrellas were very much up and in front again in the 1914–18 war. Writing of the atrocious weather in the trenches, Major Le Sinkinson said, 'The remedy was at hand, the temptation overpowering and the example infectious. The Company survived the shock of my "unsoldierly conduct" and after a time the front line began to look like a palid imitation of a wet day at Ascot. The ferrules were a sore temptation to German snipers, but otherwise the casualty rate was not increased.' Nearby Armentières was as famous for its brollies sold at 2 fr. 75 cents as for its *Mesdemoiselles.*

Of the build-up to the Second World War, Jessica Mitford said, 'The discreet, impervious men of the Cliveden set, with their furled umbrellas, so symbolic of furled minds, came and went on their missions to the embattled areas and said little.' The umbrella went on to become forever associated with the delusion of 'peace with honour', and when war came, means and methods waged rendered it impotent.

As to that implacable enemy, the weather, battles continue to be won and lost; the umbrella is a true defence against the cats and dogs of the English and the little shoemaker boys of the Danes – and yet, according to Lowell, of 'no avail against a Scotch mist'.

Eighteen

METAPHORICAL

THE first metaphorical umbrella was put up by John Donne, who was born in the early 1570s and died in 1631. 'We have an earthly cave, our bodies, to go in to by consideration, and cool ourselves; and . . . we have within us a torch, a soul, lighter and warmer than any without; we are therefore our own umbrellas and our own suns.'

It was a few years yet before the rain was to fall, but it had started to do so by the time the umbrella metaphor was applied to plants. This was roughly about the same time as the Plague and the Great Fire. Today we are very familiar with *umbelliferae* in our vegetable patches and our kitchens – carrots, parsnips and such-like, all so called because they have flat flowers, reminiscent of the flat umbrellas which were fashionable in the seventeenth century. The cursed ground elder is one of the family too, although its Latin name translates to 'goat and little foot', describing its leaves and not its umbrella-shaped flowers. Ground elder has lots of other nicknames too, one of which is Herb Gerard, although that has nothing to do with John Gerard who was famous for a *Herbal* published in 1597 – 'not unprofitable though unpolished', he said. Ground elder is nicknamed after Saint Gerard, who answered the prayers of gouty old monks in the Middle Ages. Culpeper later said that the plant could be used to cure sciatica and 'joint-ache'. All you had to do was cook it like spinach or brew it up as tea.

Another edible umbrella, although more accurately a parasol, is the mushroom *hepiota*. It comes in two sizes, *procera*, which grows nearly 12 in high and has a cap which can be 7 in across, and *rhacodes*, with a cap not much bigger than half the size. The former grows in groups at the edges of copses or in woodland clearings. The surface of the cap has shaggy brown scales which form a kind of fringe round the perimeter. The gills are white. The stem is at first rather like brown felt, but as it grows it splits into a kind of crocodile appearance and that makes it tough to eat. The smaller *rhacodes* remains smooth and white. It can be found in woods, but likes a richer soil. In fact it can be grown on the compost heap in the garden. When picked, the cap turns a reddish colour, but it tastes delicious.

There are a lot of close relations in the saxifrage family but each has a central stalk and an umbrella of large round leaves. Beware if you have only a patio or a pond in the garden though, for the Royal Horticultural Society declares the family 'very invasive'.

There's more room in Madagascar however for umbrella grass. Its ribs are about 18 in long and they are crowned with rosettes of long, arching bracts. It has a certain sophistication about it too, for it comes in two sets of colours with matching ribs and bracts, dark green, or green-and-white striped.

Passé sophisticated perhaps is the umbrella plant for open-plan offices. Originally a native of Queensland, it is resistant to neglect and doesn't mind a bit of stuffiness. Even without much care, every now and then a little clenched hand of new leaves will emerge from its single stem and then grow quickly with drooping lilt to end in six to eight large glossy leaves.

Even more resistant to neglect is the umbrella pine of Japan, which will become a giant some 100 ft high if left on its own, or can provide oakum, a fibrous sort of thing rather like old rope which was used for caulking – stuffing the seams of ships – or as the *Oxford English Dictionary* says for 'stopping leaks'. The degree of resistance its timbers show is borne out by the Sensu Bridge in Tokyo which lasted for over three hundred years without a coat of paint. Tough stuff when one remembers that its umbrella sobriquet comes from the shoots at the tip of its twigs which circle out with all the daintiness of a lady's parasol.

The flat-topped umbrella thorn, also used to make matting, doesn't grow so big, but lives for over three hundred years if left alone in its native Africa. The Americans, of course, have an umbrella tree too. It grows to over a hundred feet and has relations in many other parts as do so many Americans, this one being a magnolia. The mighty Texans have a special one all to themselves that grows to about 70 ft, but makes up for its comparative lack of size with lilac-like, scented flowers and yellow berries.

It was not until Victorian days that the umbrella became associated with marine life. First there was the jellyfish, a ubiquitous sort of family who don't mind much where in the world they live, although the ones in our Mediterranean playgrounds might not easily recognize cousin *cvanae aretica*. It is brilliantly blue and measures some 6 ft across. Jellyfish of all sorts work on the same principle; they have a sort of transparent umbrella with cells above and below. Those below are for digesting food; those above for protection. The umbrella in the middle looks like a wobbly jelly but it is remarkably solid, and the jellyfish *in toto* either floats along pretty motionless near the surface of the sea or goes for a swim by contracting the muscles of the cells on the top of its

umbrella. There is a choice of seventeen different types of cell, both above and below the umbrella, from which to sting and replacements are quickly grown for ones used up.

Another watery character is the 6 in long Mediterranean Lam snail. Its round umbrella shell is slightly dented, or concave, just about where its neck sticks out. It is not the handsomest of creatures for it has a lot of yellow and reddish warts round its tummy, poor thing.

Perhaps the weather is what the umbrella bird, commonly called the Chatterer, talks about. He is after all a very sophisticated bird. To begin with, he's black. And he only eats fruit. There's no messy digging for worms. He dresses when he goes out courting – he puts up his umbrella crest. On his card, it would say *Cephalopterus* from the family *Cotingidae* of the order of *Passeriformas*.

There are three half-brothers in the family. The most spectacular lives in Ecuador or Colombia and he has an inflatable wattle, so he's known as *C. Penduliger*. His appendage is covered with black feathers, and if he feels so inclined, he can inflate it to a length of more than 2 ft. *C. Ornatus*, whose address is the Amazon basin, has a shorter wattle but to compensate he can inflate it into a sort of triangle, although the hindside is devoid of feathers. Brother *C. Glabricollis* stays away in Panama or Costa Rica, for, poor chap, by comparison with the others, his wattle is short, bare and red.

✶ The French made an 'aeroplane umbrella' to celebrate Bleriot's crossing the Channel. Two shorter ribs produced the wing shape.

✶ A martyr to dyspepsia, he [Mr Phippen] used the lightest umbrella he could pick out of the hall as a sunshade.

WILKIE COLLINS
The Dead Secret

✶ The Chinese, when they walk abroad, carry a small Umbrella in their hands, wherewith they fence their head from The Sun or The Rain.

WILLIAM DAMPIER
Voyages

✶ Lean old hags, like worn umbrellas with a quivering bonnet on top.

KATHERINE MANSFIELD
The Garden Party

✶ Blest was the prophet in his heavenly shade
But ah! how soon did his umbrella fade!
Like our frail bodys, which being born of clay,
Spring in a night and wither in a day.

*Epitaph for John Boyle,
who died at Barnstaple in 1684 aged six years*

✶ Simpson's of Piccadilly's 1937 budget of £50 for the well-dressed man included an umbrella at a cost of 1 gn and a business suit for 5gns. A budget of £115 allowed two business suits at 8 gns each and an umbrella at £1 15s.

✶ The Umbrella Garden Tent with Sloping Walls.

*Advertised by the Army and Navy
Co-operative Society (1895)*

Nineteen

SPORTING

I S it not strange to see so little brollyball played these days? Many city alleys have survived the bulldozer to remain ready pitches. The balls, just a little heavier than those used by Henry V, rise not to window level; nor do they split the curved cane of the reversed brolly. The intricacy of scoring is no problem now that numeracy demands no more than the possession of a pocket calculator.

The oldest of umbrella sports is a kind of archery, narrated in a Japanese tale from the sixteenth century. It was the sort of thing William Tell would have been good at, for the Japanese aimed to split the umbrella shaft.

One of the newer sports is balancing the brolly on the proboscis. Current champion is Mr Leo Birchir, who for more than two and a half hours lay prostrate with a heavy golf umbrella upon his nose. He achieved this remarkable feat in Switzerland's small town of Zug, which has few claims to fame other than hosting the 1982 World Record Breakers Championships.

It was reported that competitors 'pushed themselves to their limits' to attain the joy of 'pure concentration' in 'surpassing goals'. There is some doubt as to whether Mr Birchir can be classified as a dedicated sportsman however, for at the end of the event he slid quickly and quietly away, murmuring that he had had 'a simply unadulterated craving to balance things since childhood'. His performance left him with a nose 'flattened for most of Saturday' and 'red', a hue which could have been more joyfully acquired perhaps at a feast of Bacchus or from indulgence in spiced cake.

> Nose, nose, jolly red nose,
> And who gave thee this jolly red nose?
> Nutmegs and ginger, cinnamon and cloves,
> And they gave me this jolly red nose.

Sport tends to be equated with exercise, although Jerrold

claimed that 'the only athletic sport [he] ever mastered was backgammon.' Pooh wasn't exactly doing much either when he went afloat in a sort of a boat, i.e. an upturned umbrella. Nor had Robinson Crusoe got the sailing business quite sorted out, using his umbrella 'in a step at the stern, like a mast, to stand over my head, and keep the heat of the sun off like an awning.'

It wasn't until 1844 that Lieutenant Halkett made a sort of lifeboat with an umbrella for a sail, but he also took a paddle along with him just in case. Captain Bayton was next, sailing from Westminster to Greenwich with nothing more than an ebbing tide and an umbrella in 1875. Acceptability of the technique came with the publication of Smyth's *Sailors' Word Book* in 1876 which had the following entry:

> *Umbrella warping*: a contrivance similar to our umbrella, by which ships in a calm sea can be warped ahead.

Twenty years later, *The Mariners' Mirror* reported on an umbrella rig. 'The sail when spread had precisely the appearance of a large open umbrella, the mast of the boat forming the stick.'

Apart from being capsize-proof – 'the sail had no tendency to keel the boat over' according to *Pearson's Magazine* in 1900 – the umbrella sail also had the advantage that it 'can be set or furled in a minute [even though] it does not close up as does an umbrella, but each side shuts up like a fan.' Had all this happened during the lifetime of Robert Louis Stevenson, perhaps he would have adapted:

> The rain is raining all around
> It falls on field and tree,
> It rains on the umbrella here,
> And on the ships at sea.

People have not just gone along with umbrellas; a good many have come down with them. The women who jumped from the Kiyomizu temple to draw the attention of their gods to their prayers were not so sure of heavenly protection that they didn't open their parasols to soften their fall. Chinese Emperor Shun imprisoned his son in a tower and then set fire to it. Being less well equipped than most Chinese, the son jumped with nothing more than his conical

hat, which you could say was the next best thing to an umbrella, or indeed was simply an umbrella fastened down by a bow under his chin.

There was a half-way stage between going along and dropping down at the end of the seventeenth century. Simon de la Loubère reported that the Siamese court jester tied umbrellas to his belt to make 'great leaps'; presumably the jest did not include using the many-tiered ritual umbrellas from the king's audience chamber.

Large, but simple, was the umbrella with a diameter of $7\frac{1}{2}$ ft which Montgolfier made in 1779. He took it up a tower, tied a sheep in the basket underneath, and pushed the whole thing off. Blanchard repeated the experiment two years later with a 23 ft-wide brolly and a dog. In 1783 Sebastian le Normand made the first human drop. Blanchard then had a go himself, and liked it enough to repeat several times. In the narrative of his *3rd Aerial Voyage*, on which he was accompanied by a M. Boby, Blanchard records that when they were down to a hundred feet from the ground, the local peasants called up to ask whether they were 'Men, or gods?'

In 1784 a treatise for balloonists was published under the title *Hints on Aerostatic Globes*. It recommended that balloonists should take ordinary, everyday umbrellas with them in order to slow their descent should they be forced to abandon their craft.

Sporting under forced circumstances was General Bournouville, who jumped 40 ft from Olmutz prison in 1793. Descending with brolly, the only injury he sustained was a broken leg.

Jumping for pleasure in 1838 was John Hampton, who, with an umbrella 15 ft in diameter, dropped 9,000 ft from a balloon over Cheltenham. It took him fifteen minutes to reach the ground. Cheltenham has probably never seen anything quite like it since, although gentlemen may now watch the umbrella set of fielders on that most English of greens, the cricket pitch.

Some two hundred years ago, sport was defined as 'a pleasant pastime, an amusement, a diversion'. A modern master of verbal sport was Paul Jennings, who got up one morning feeling 'a little Wembley'. The student of the umbrella will know Rainhill Stoops Esq., who felt as Umberleigh as Mr Jennings felt Wembley. Stooping to pick up his Bromley from the Raynes Park in the hall, Rainhill could see many passers-by who were already Undy, but he pushed the Upper Poppleton button on his brolly and went to inspect the Rainsworth at the bottom of the garden to measure the night's fall. He felt a little more Coveney at the thought of not having to get the watering can out when he returned from the office later that day, and dreamt for a second that should Rainscough during the day and the sun come out, a few frivolous moments in the garden under the Paris-sol with his new lady love might be the order of play.

Twenty

PAPAL

F RESCOES showing scenes from the lives of St Sylvester, Pope from AD 314 to 335, and Emperor Constantine were painted in what is now known as the Oratory of St Sylvester in the convent adjoining the SS Quattro Coronati church in Rome in the twelfth century. A red and yellow striped *ombrellino* can be seen being handed over to the saint who is to be left in charge of the West while the emperor goes off to his new capital, Constantinople. That story is, however, disputed by those who say that Constantine had suffered from leprosy and arranged for the brolly to be passed over as a sign of thanksgiving for his recovery, and by others who say that it was just common practice to keep brollies in basilicas to protect visiting kings and princes from weather fair or foul and hence one just happened to be around.

For three or four hundred years after Sylvester, depictions of the *ombrellino* varied from being roundly open to half-closed and the stripes from roundabout to vertical. Colours were nearly always yellow and red, though a fifteenth-century depiction in Bologna, which looks more like a bell-tent, had blue and gold stripes on the 'roof' and red and gold on the sides.

Coronation expenses of early popes included a quantity of green linen, believed to have been for relining the papal umbrella for Innocent VI in 1353, and silver for repairing the angel attached to that of Sixtus IV in 1471.

Eugenius IV (1431–47), who was driven out of Rome and spent most of his papacy in Tuscany, incorporated an *ombrellino* in his coat of arms, but just over fifty years later the *ombrellino*, together with crossed keys, became the emblem of temporal power. This happened when Alexander VI encouraged his son Caesare Borgia to establish the Papal States as a political entity in their own right. Caesare Borgia incorporated the motif on his seal in 1502. Other early examples of its temporal use are to be found on tiles in the castle of

St Angelo in Rome and in the windows of the Laurentian Library in Florence. In the seventeenth century, Urban VIII's nephew, Taddeo Barberini, used the motif on a marble fireplace in St Angelo to separate the Barberini bees from the Colonna column of his wife's coat of arms and Urban's brother had it put on his tomb, this time with the bees buzzing around it.

The papal was not the first mint to use *ombrellini* on its coins. When Herod Agrippa was King of Judaea from AD 37–44 one side of his coins showed an umbrella.

Heliogabalus, the early third-century Roman emperor, had umbrellas on his medallions.

The church didn't come in until 1521, when a coin was struck to commemorate the interregnum following the death of Leo X. From then on the interregnum coin became a habit which continues until the present day. There were strikes for both Paul VI's death in 1978 and again a few weeks later on the death of John Paul I.

The heraldic *ombrellino* is now used by the Sacred College of Cardinals, the Apostolic Chamber, and by certain institutions and seminaries. From the seventeenth century it has been used by families who render particular service to a pope or provide a pope. It is also seen on buildings completed during an interregnum. It is never now used by the Pope himself.

Basilicas, which until the nineteenth century existed only in Rome, may use the heraldic *ombrellino*. Interestingly, the German for *ombrellino* is *basilikaschirm*. Processions in major basilicas have *ombrellini* decorated with tiara and crossed keys; minor basilicas have a plainer version. Both are of yellow and red silk.

🎋 'Brolliology' was coined in 1952 by a geographer studying what he called 'a private and perambulent oasis'.

🎋 A pleasant old buffer, nephew to a lord,
  Who believed that the bank was mightier than
    the sword,
  And that an umbrella might pacify barbarians
    abroad,
  Just like an old Liberal between the wars.

WILLIAM PLOMER

🎋 She asked for a husband as if he was an umbrella. She mislaid him on Saturday afternoon – and for a long time suffered no inconvenience.

E.M. FORSTER
Howard's End

🎋 The soft humidity of the evening, so pleasant to walk about in earlier, had turned to rain. The strolling tourists had melted away. One or two people hurried by under umbrellas. This is what the inhabitants who live here see, he thought. This is the true life. Empty streets by night, the dank stillness of a stagnant canal beneath shuttered houses. The rest is a bright façade put on for show, glittering by sunlight.

DAPHNE DU MAURIER
on Venice (Don't Look Now)

🎋 Here lie the bones of Brother Connolly
  Who one day forgot to go out with his brolly.
  When it rained cats and dogs
  He sank into his clogs,
  And rests here regretting his folly.

ANON

Twenty-One

ELEVATED

TO the Quaker the umbrella is a symbol of meek-
ness, but the Egyptian hieroglyphic drawn like an
open umbrella meant sovereignty. Gods, kings,
chieftains and popes all have them.

The priests of the sun and of Poseidon and Athena walked
to the temple under large white umbrellas.

The Chinese used them as a symbol of rank in the
eleventh century BC. The frames were of cane or sandalwood
and the covers of leather or feathers, presumably for wet and
dry days. In the first century AD they were attaching brollies
to chariots they were racing to the gods of thunder and wind
as a tribute to divinity. During the Ming dynasty of 1368–
1644 there were still elaborate laws governing the grade of
umbrella certain subjects might use.

Buddha adopted the umbrella as one of his eight symbols;
hence the solar wheel over his head.

Emperor Darius went out for his constitutional in Perse-
polis, donning a top hat and followed by his umbrella bearer.

Popes proceeded under them, minted them, and gave
them away as presents.

In Turkey the palace sentries dipped theirs as a mark of
respect for the sultan.

In the thirteenth century, a Burmese king who couldn't
make up his mind as to which of his five sons he should
bequeath the crown, stood them in a circle and put his
umbrella in the middle. The prince towards whom it fell
would become king. The lucky one got nicknamed
Tilominlo, which meant 'the king whom the umbrella placed
on the throne' – at least that is what is supposed. As late as
1855, there was still in the title of his descendants: 'The
glorious and most excellent Majesty of Burma, King of the
White Elephants and Lord of the twenty-four umbrellas.' It
can only be hoped that after all that time a use had been
found for the white elephants too.

Even in Europe the umbrella was considered so important

to royalty that it was listed among the items which Catherine de Medici brought with her when she arrived to marry the future Henry II in 1533. Louis XIII was quite a collector too, purchasing Turkish and German umbrellas to use on sunny days. He also had three 'oil-skin umbrellas' for when it was less fine, but even they were reputed to be trimmed with gold and silver lace.

The *Oxford English Dictionary* does in fact date the use of the word umbrella from 1653 as 'an Oriental or African symbol of dignity'. The English may have been a little ignorant of the role it played in Africa though, until a certain Mr Bowdich got to the land of the Asante in 1817. He was met by 'at least a hundred large umbrellas, which could [each] shelter thirty persons. [The umbrellas] were sprung up and down by the bearers with brilliant effect.' Those he saw were most likely of plain red cloth, although a kind of yellow velvet might also have been used. Very important chiefs would have multi-coloured nasa cloth, which was made from sheep or goat wool. Some were even of leopard skin. The umbrellas had valances, sometimes scalloped and/or fringed, and were topped by the proverbial wood carvings or by golden images. Surprisingly, the umbrellas were all made to fold up, but that did not stop the most important chiefs from sitting under them in their palaces at night. It was all to do with shielding their heads from the sight of their gods.

Asante-land was not the only part of Africa in which umbrellas were and still are important. In Morocco in 1844, the list of Bugeaud's spoils of war when he beat an army six times larger than his own included 'eighteen flags, eleven guns, the tent, parasol and personal correspondence of the Emperor's son.'

Much nearer our own time, a firm in Leicester made two umbrellas, each 14 ft high and 12 ft across, for Akenzua II when he was chief of the Benin in Nigeria.

Royalty today meets with the ceremonial on Commonwealth tours, but is no doubt more grateful for the practical protection than anything else. Royalty has always been pretty practical. Queen Anne was among the first of English ladies to carry a brolly, and Queen Victoria had one lined with chain-mail following an attempt to assassinate her. Presumably she was no more amused when she and Albert were caught in the rain while walking near East Cowes in 1844, but it led to an incident which showed a touching

concern for her subjects. Luckily, they met the postman. In those days, postmen usually carried bells, but this one happened to be carrying an umbrella instead. Not knowing whom he met, he offered his brolly to 'the lady'. Next morning, the *Morning Post* reported 'the old postman tendered his gingham, but perfectly waterproof, umbrella.' The Queen thoughtfully not only returned the borrowed brolly but wrapped a £5 note up inside it. The *Morning Post* was able to continue, 'The old letter carrier, who for more than twenty years has never had a day absent from his duty . . . expresses his intention of never more using the umbrella, but preserving it as an heirloom.' In this case, the brolly was lost to the elements.

Edward VII was allowed to show some independence of mind when he attached his umbrella to the tricycle he used for rural rides around Sandringham.

Unceremonial was the mufti Edward VIII was ordered to wear after he had joined the Guards: 'Frock coat, top hat, with a tight umbrella.' The adjutant not only had the right of sartorial direction over his subalterns, but the right of direction to a tailor of his own choice. It is not known how this affected the royal warrant, but so many princes and peers were in the Guards that the tight umbrella became a sort of *ex officio* badge once they returned to civvies.

Princess Mary was also never to be seen without an umbrella, winter or summer. It was ignominiously nicknamed by her brothers 'Mary's twin'.

The word 'modest' will soon become like the word 'honourable', which is said to be employed by the Japanese before any word that occurs in a polite sentence, as 'Put honourable umbrella in honourable umbrella-stand.'

G.K. CHESTERTON
The Worship of the Wealthy

The summer sun was never on the street but in the morning about breakfast-time, when it came with the water-carts and the old-clothes man, and the people with geraniums, and the umbrella- mender, and the man who trilled the little bell of the Dutch clock as he went along.

CHARLES DICKENS
Dombey and Son

On a wet and windy day
Sarah kept the rain at bay.
Raising gamp by ten degrees –
At least she kept it off her knees.
Sadly though in bed that night
She did have an awful fright.
For Ah-Ah-Tishoo! Dreadful sneezes
Emanate from nose not kneezes.

ANON

Uncle Henry Hamilton 'marched in the rank behind Grandpa Merriwether. . . . Beside him marched his black valet, who was nearly as old as Uncle Henry, with an open umbrella held over them both.'

MARGARET MITCHELL
Gone With the Wind

Twenty-Two

CHILDREN'S

ONCE upon a time there were party games, Musical Chairs, Pass the Parcel, and so on. Among them was 'I went to market with a green umbrella'. Each child in turn named a purchase and the one who could repeat the longest list won the prize. It is unlikely that it is played today, the computer having made memory as redundant as multiplication tables.

Christmas crackers survive:

Three large women went walking under one umbrella, but none of them got wet. Why not?
It wasn't raining.

What will go up the chimney down, but not down the chimney up?

And so do rhymes:

'Cheep, cheep cheep, what horrid rain',
Cried three little ducks in a country lane.
'We shan't get home with one dry feather,
Did you ever see such awful weather?'

'Quack! Quack! Quack!' cried master duck,
'Rain and puddles! Oh what luck!
I must be quite a different fella,
You won't catch me with a silly umbrella.'

And then there is the 'gooseberry-bush' element, though in this case harmless and maybe with even a small grain of truth:

'Where is my toadstool?' loud he lamented.
And that's how umbrellas were first invented.

119

Children's rhymes about umbrellas tend to be funny. Stories used to be serious and with a moral.

Amelia-Anne's mother was so poor that she took in washing. (Middle-class children tended to think that that meant it had come on to rain.) Invited to a party, Amelia-Anne stuffed her umbrella with goodies to take home to her hungry brothers and sisters, but, alas, as she left the party it was raining, and some well-meaning grown-up opened up the umbrella to help her. The other children laughed as the booty dropped to the ground, but the understanding adults packed a large hamper.

There is no moral in the 1920s tale of Gladys Conk, although it might now almost be seen as educational, concerning life in the big city. Gladys Conk was a nurserymaid, and the mother of her charge, Milly, gave Gladys a new umbrella for Christmas. 'It had a duck's-head handle made of imitation silver and she always took it for walks with her and it was a good thing she did because of the robber.' Refusing his demand for money, Gladys bashed him with her brolly and killed him. Not a very nice story perhaps for little girls like Milly, although it did have a happy ending. Gladys married the policeman who arrested her. 'They had six children; five girls and one little policeman.'

Images from childhood tend to stick. Father Brown, who has wandered ubiquitously through the tale of the umbrella, 'found himself eyeing the knobbed and clumsy head of his own shabby umbrella with some fair memories of the ogre's club in a coloured toy-book.'

The mature men of the Meteorological Office commented during the gale of January 1990 that 'You would be nuts to put up an umbrella in these conditions unless you are Mary Poppins.'

Umbrellas have survived far more in children's literature over the last fifty years or so than they have in adult's, although moralizing, along with games of memory training, has gone. Almost anti-moral is the story of the lost umbrella which preferred to remain hidden, warm and dry, in the tea-chest of the lost property office, missing the storm, although admittedly its inexperienced replacement displayed a certain degree of shock that it should be so.

While we relax with stories of sex and violence and wonder who dunit?, children's stories retain an innocence which frequently seems to come out as fantasy. In *The Magic*

Umbrella, the wizard left (we might say 'lost'!) his umbrella in the market-place. The farmer's wife who found it and took it home didn't realize that it responded to magic numbers. Say 'three' quite by chance, and the umbrella whisked you home immediately. Say 'five', and you were immediately transported to wherever you most wanted to be at that particular moment. Say 'seven', and there you were floating round the top of the nearest church spire. Mary Poppins's umbrella at least left her behind when it floated up over the garden gate or up over the bannisters. Maybe it is the element of fantasy which has led Mary Poppins to live on while Gladys Conk has died.

The gooseberry-bush factor survives too – in planting umbrellas in gardens to grow into umbrella trees – but perhaps the most striking thing about children's literature is that it seems essential for there to be a happy-ever-after ending. Even the farmer's wife got over her ordeal after a couple of weeks in bed. Do the authors have the dreams of bedtime in mind? With no need to remember things, no need to count, is fantasy all that is left? In a world still bursting with sin and sorrow, do the problems come so soon that nonsense is good while you can get it?

Nonsense is so difficult to judge. There are those who think it is going to be a far funnier thing if the Californians can ever prove that Queen Victoria wrote *Alice* – she did so like underlining words – than anything they can get out of Lewis Carroll. There is great visual fun when Alice asks Tweedledee if he thinks it is going to rain. 'No, I don't think it is, at least not under here. No how!' at which point he gets himself in rather a pickle trying to shut the umbrella up around him. 'But it may rain outside', said Alice. 'It may if it chooses, we've no objection. Contrariwise.'

Other examples of Dodgson's work leave one with a bit of a problem. When he was about seventeen or eighteen, he produced a magazine called *The Rectory Umbrella* for his brothers and sisters. One of the covers was a pretty serious comment on life. An 'old feller' sat under an umbrella whose panels were marked 'tales, poetry, fun, riddles and jokes'. So far, so good. Coming to his aid were good humour, liveliness, knowledge, mirth, content, cheerfulness and taste. Still good. But, attacking him were evil spirits such as woe and spite. Contrariwise?

More straightforward was the serial he wrote for his

magazine. Sadly for us, it was called *The Walking Stick of Destiny*, but from time to time there were umbrellas about:

> All day he sat without a hat
> The comical old feller,
> Shading his form from the driving storm
> With the rectory umbrella.

and many more verses until:

> But the wine had left the cellar,
> And I hear the dinner bell,
> So fare thee well, my old umbrella,
> Dear umbrella, fare thee well.

Twenty-Three

SUBSTITUTES

WITH umbelliferous vegetation readily available in many parts of the world, imagination needs little stretching to find a perfectly good substitute for the umbrella. Moreover, if an umbrella is a potential loss-maker anyway, why worry about ephemerality? On a rainy day the herbaceous in the hand is worth a couple of cotton in the closet.

J. Davies was one of the first (in 1662) to record just how useful leaves can be, and not just for umbrellas. 'Of leaves they make sayles, they make of them likewise umbrelloes, fans, tents, mats and hats.'

It is a fashion that has weathered time. Sir Frank Cooper's *Friar Park Guide*, published at the end of the nineteenth century, pictured some Japanese gentlemen sheltering their shoulders under leaves of *petasites japonicus*. With leaves as large as 4 ft in diameter and handles up to 6 ft long, *PJ* made excellent cover.

Swift saw more originality among Protestant dissenters of his acquaintance, claiming that a document of parchment could serve us as 'an umbrella in rainy weather and a night-cap for bedtime'.

A more mundane, though readily to hand, substitute formed part of a striking outfit for Isabella Bird in the 1870s. Isabella could have been a heroine of romantic Victorian fiction. Daughter of a clergyman, small of stature, cursed with a spinal tumour, she seemed made for a life of langour on the drawing-room sofa. Instead, she set off for Hawaii. Finding she could ride comfortably only if astride a Mexican-type, man's saddle, she got herself some fully frilled Turkish-type trousers, but for modesty's sake covered them with a tartan flannel skirt that reached to her ankles. 'A broad-brimmed Australian hat served the double purpose of sunshade and umbrella,' she wrote. Other accessories included jangling Mexican spurs and a lei of orange *pandamus* seeds.

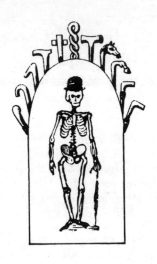

Twenty-Four

LAMENT

THE bus of today is but a moving advertisement. No longer is the upstairs outside. No longer does the conductor call 'Anyone on top?' as he watches the descent of 'an errant umbrella point and the hem of a mackintosh'. Journeying encapsulated in cars, we park as near as we can to the lift that goes down to the dry-shod mall. Computer-linked plastic sweeps through the checkouts. No brolly is needed to vouch for status.

Brolly-bashing, though still practised by commuters in Paris when some stupid foreigner jams the automatic gates on the Metro, is no longer sufficient force for the political demo, and wars of the world will be fought by a push-button far from the *pi-chi*.

As we have put our heads above the *parapluie*, so we have exposed our bodies. From one-piece to two-, from two-piece to bikini and naturism. There is no longer a 'stickler for appearances' such as Robert Siddons with his bowler hat and umbrella in Honolulu.

Femininity has turned into an *ism* – and slain the gallant in the process.

The satellite dish is our only mirror to St Medard.

Is there nothing left but the umbelliferous hemlock of 'the idle weeds that grow in our sustaining corn'?

Cover for umbrageous practices?

The collective noun as we participate in the Umbrella Forum of the Community Programme and invest in Umbrella Funds?

But, 'if you took away everything in the world that had to be invented, there'd be nothing left except a lot of people getting rained on,' said Tom Stoppard. *Can* the umbrella, with its myths and magic, protect us yet from the 'sorrowful' but no doubt very wet 'countenance . . . of these crocodile tears'?

Dear Umbrella, fare thee well.

COMPANION UMBRELLA